FAMOUS
WEXFORDIANS

FAMOUS WEXFORDIANS

Liam Gaul

Cover illustrations: front: Sir Robert John Le Mesurier McClure & Eileen Gray in later years, *back:* Jem Roche, Irish Heavyweight Champion in fighting pose (Courtesy of the Roche family) & Anita Lett, founder of the ICA.

First published 2019

The History Press
The Mill, Brimscombe Port
Stroud, Gloucestershire, GL5 2QG
www.thehistorypress.co.uk

© Liam Gaul, 2019

The right of Liam Gaul to be identified as the Author
of this work has been asserted in accordance with the
Copyright, Designs and Patents Act 1988.

British Library Cataloguing in Publication Data.
A catalogue record for this book is available from the British Library.

ISBN 978 0 7509 8907 7

Typesetting and origination by The History Press
Printed and bound in Great Britain by TJ International Ltd

CONTENTS

To all Wexfordians over the centuries who brought notoriety to their native county, whether at home or abroad, in the activities that brought success and satisfaction, whether in pursuits on land, sea, sport or in entrepreneurial endeavours, in an effort to find a better and more rewarding life.

ABOUT THE AUTHOR

A native of Wexford town, Liam Gaul has a lifelong interest in history and is a regular contributor to various journals and newspapers. His lectures to historical societies, schools and other groups, together with his summer radio series on South East Radio, are an important part of his activities. He is currently researching a further book of historical and musical interest. Liam is president of the Wexford Historical Society, and a member of the Wexford Gramophone Society. He is a graduate of the University of Limerick, the National University of Ireland (Maynooth) and the Open University.

ACKNOWLEDGEMENTS

I wish to thank the following: Breda Banville, ICA; Gloria Hurley-Binions; Jane Cantwell; Brian Cleare; Philip Corish, Michael Dempsey and the staff at Local Studies, Wexford Library; Gráinne Doran, archivist, Wexford County Archive; Marion Doyle, SIPTU; Danny Forde; James Gaul, Cobh; Jarlath Glynn; Brendan Howlin, T.D.; Ken Hemmingway; Susan Kelly, Library Headquarters; Angela Laffan, district manager, Wexford Borough District; Denise O'Connor-Murphy; David McLoughlin, CEO Wexford Festival Opera; Aidan Quirke; Padge Reck; Billy Roche; Nicky Rossiter; Aidan Ryan, Brownswood, Enniscorthy; Eithne Scallan; Seamus Seery; Mary Somers, ICA; Catherine Walsh, SIPTU; David Williams; Dominic Williams; Helen Corish-Wylde, the Friday Historians. To my publisher, The History Press Ireland. Finally, my sincere thanks to my wife and family for their interest, support and patience.

Photographic credits: Denise O'Connor-Murphy; Pat Sheridan; Aidan Ryan; Aidan Quirke, Helen Corish-Wylde, National Gallery of Ireland, Matt Wheeler, Irish Agricultural Museum Archive, Johnstown Castle, Paddy Berry, Tesco, Wexford, Enniscorthy Museum, Brian Cleare.

INTRODUCTION

Many of County Wexford's sons and daughters have brought fame and glory on themselves and their native place over the past decades. I have included profiles of some of them in *Famous Wexfordians*. Three of them, although not born in the county – namely our national poet Thomas Moore, through his mother; master musician, composer and organist William Henry Grattan Flood, who lived the greater part of his life in Enniscorthy; and Anita Lett, founder of a national women's organisation – we claim as Wexfordians. The United States recognised Commodore John Barry as Father of the American Navy, and the man who discovered the Northwest Passage, Sir Robert McClure, was born on Wexford's Main Street. In the struggle for freedom, Wexfordians took up arms during the Insurrection of 1798, and again during the First World War in answer to John Redmond's call for Irishmen to fight in Belgium and France, all with great loss of life. Known as the Model County for its rich and productive land, a far-seeing James Pierce gained world renown for his manufacture of agricultural machinery. Remnants of an ancient language spoken in the south-east of the county were collected by Jacob Poole, and from the coastal areas Fr Joseph Ranson preserved songs in print of wreck and rescue. It was folklorist Patrick Kennedy who recounted the many legends and stories in his excellent publications. Art and music, both traditional and operatic, came to the fore with the *uilleann* piping of the Rowsomes, and the internationally proclaimed festival of opera founded by Dr Tom Walsh and the artistic work of the multitalented artist, designer and author, Eileen Gray from Brownswood, Enniscorthy are profiled here. County Wexford was well represented in sporting activities such as hurling and boxing, with such heroes as hurler supreme, Nickey Rackard, and blacksmith pugilist, Jem Roche. In the past, many castles and fine manor houses, occupied by the landed gentry, were dotted across the county, with only one castle occupied today and Johnstown Castle in a stage of refurbishment. Religion and politics are covered with the story of Fr James Roche, builder of the twin churches in the county town, and the Corish family who served the people in local and national politics for eighty-four years. I trust *Famous Wexfordians* will give an insight into the lives of some of those men and women included in my book. Enjoy.

Liam Gaul
2019

— 1 —

FATHER OF THE AMERICAN NAVY

Commodore John Barry

Commodore John Barry lived an exciting life as a sailor and soldier during the American Revolution and in the formative years of the United States of America, which afforded him some signal honours in its naval service. John Frost (1800–59) writes of John Barry:

> The career of this distinguished officer commences with the infancy of our navy, and is marked by many brilliant services. His name occurs in connection with not a few of the more remarkable events in the history of the revolutionary war, and always with credit to himself, and honour to the flag under which he sailed. Few commanders in the navy were employed in a greater variety of service, or met the enemy under greater disadvantages. Yet, in no one of the numerous actions in which he was engaged, did Commodore Barry ever fail to acquit himself of his duty in a manner becoming a skilful seaman and an able warrior.[1]

John Barry was born in 1745 at Ballysampson in the Parish of Tacumshin.[2] His father was a tenant farmer evicted by his English landlord, forcing the family to relocate to Rosslare. It was here that young Barry got his love of the sea from his father's brother, Nicholas Barry, who was captain of a fishing skiff. John was determined at an early age to follow his uncle to sea. From a ship's cabin boy he graduated from seaman to able-seaman and, eventually, achieved a mate's rating. Barry grew to be an imposing man of almost 6ft 4in, of muscular build and a well-respected seaman. His height was determined by Rear Admiral G.H. Preble (1816–85), naval historian, who examined John Barry's Federal Navy uniform which dated from the 1790s.[3]

John Barry was held in very high esteem in the services of his adopted country in a bid for her freedom. The young Barry went to Spanishtown in Jamaica, and from there sailed to Philadelphia. Besides Philadelphia's growing population, the city was also emerging as a great maritime trade centre. It was from Philadelphia that Barry gained his early skills of command at the helm of several merchant ships plying back and forth between his home port and the West Indies. 'Big John', as he was popularly known to Philadelphians, was noted for his reliability and personable nature.

He soon became much sought after in the merchant shipping business. He was just 21 years of age when he took command of the 60-ton schooner *Barbados* leaving Philadelphia on 2 October 1766. The schooner was owned by Edward Denny of Philadelphia and was built at Liverpool, Nova Scotia. John Barry was registered as its captain. Barry served as captain on several vessels, taking charge of the brig *Patty and Polly* in May 1771, sailing from St Croix to Philadelphia, and in August of that year captained the schooner *Industry*, a 45-tonner sailing to and from Virginia with trips to New York and to Halifax, Nova Scotia. Later, in October 1772, he took command of the *Peggy* sailing to and from St Eustatia and Montserrat. It was John Nixon, owner of the *Black Prince*, whose grandfather, Richard, had settled in Philadelphia in 1686 from Wexford, who issued a register to John Barry to act as the ship's master.

By 1772, Barry's abilities as a ship's master had come to the attention of Meredith and Clymer, one of Philadelphia's premier mercantile houses, who offered him command of the vessel *Peg*. Later, Barry transferred to the shipping firm of Willing, Morris and Cadwaladar, who gave Barry command of the 200-ton ship *Black Prince*. It was on this vessel that John Barry made the amazing and unparalleled record of travelling 237 miles by dead-reckoning in a twenty-four-hour period, giving Barry the fastest day of sailing recorded in the eighteenth century. This recorded distance happened during a voyage from England back home to America.[4]

Postage stamps issued by An Post.

On the outbreak of war between the colonies and England, Barry was given the very important task of outfitting the first Continental Navy ships which put to sea from Philadelphia. He was responsible for overseeing the rigging, piercing gun-ports, strengthening bulwarks, procuring gunpowder and canvas for the new warships, and loading provisions. Barry received a captain's commission in the Continental Navy, dated 7 December 1775 and signed by the President of Congress, John Hancock. With this commission went command of John Barry's first warship, the frigate *Lexington*. The young Wexford man was just 31 years of age.

The *Lexington* was 86ft in length with a 24ft beam, and was armed with fourteen 4-pounders, two 6-pounders and twelve swivel guns. Barry had a crew of 110 officers and men and was the first commander appointed under the direct authority of the Continental Congress. The *Lexington* cruised off the coast of Virginia, where Barry's ship had a successful encounter and shattered the British ship *Edward*, with several of her crew killed and wounded. Barry lost two men killed and two wounded. The battered *Edward* was brought to Philadelphia by Captain Barry with her commander, Lieutenant Richard Boger, and the crew of twenty-five prisoners. This was the first armed vessel taken under the authority of the Continental Marine Committee, proving that the colonies had the ability to contest the sea against Great Britain. The *Edward* was deemed by the Court of Admiralty as a prize of war. Her ammunition, furniture and tackle went to public auction, with the government and Captain Barry and his crew sharing the proceeds.

Following the encounter with the *Edward*, the *Lexington* was in need of a refit. Captain Barry sailed in the sloop *Hornet* down the Delaware River to help in the defence of the pass at Fort Island, in a bid to prevent the British coming to Philadelphia. The *Lexington* was sent down the bay to Barry to join the rest of the fleet at Cape May. With the building of thirteen ships by the Marine Committee, the thirty-two-gun frigate *Effingham* was assigned to Barry.

On 2 July 1776, the Resolution announced that the colonies were free and independent. John Hancock, President of the Congress, notified Captain Barry:

… the frigate you are to command is not yet launched, her guns and anchors not yet ready, a piece of justice due to your merit to allow you to make a cruise in the *Lexington* for one or two months, in hopes that fortune may favour your industry and reward it with some good prizes.

Fortune smiled on Captain Barry, for on 2 August he captured the *Lady Susan*, followed by the *Betsy*, bringing a share of the value to the captain and his crew. Barry commanded the *Lexington* until 18 October 1776.

As the war progressed, John Barry turned from sailor to soldier, awaiting completion of his thirty-two-gun frigate, the *Effingham*. In December 1776, Captain John Barry recruited a company of volunteers for land service and the marines cooperating with them were highly commended by General Washington. Later, Barry served as aide-de-camp to militia commander General John Cadwaladar.[5] He fought at the Battle of Trenton[6] and led a spirited defence during the Battle of

Princeton.[7] He was chosen by General Washington to convey wounded prisoners through British lines, and to carry a dispatch under a flag of truce to General Cornwallis.[8] It was the same Cornwallis who later became Lord Lieutenant of Ireland, arriving in Wexford in June during the Insurrection of 1798. Barry returned to Philadelphia and assisted in the defence of the city. When the British took possession of Philadelphia in September 1777, Barry was ordered to sail the uncompleted *Effingham* up the Delaware River for safety. On 25 October, General George Washington requested for the crew of the *Effingham* to become part of the fleet, and two days later Barry's ship was either to be sunk or burned to avoid her falling into the hands of the British. The *Effingham* was scuttled on 2 November near Bordentown, New Jersey, and was later burned at the water's edge by British forces heading northwards from Philadelphia.

The destruction of the *Effingham* left Barry without a command. On 30 May 1778, the Marine Committee appointed him to the command of the thirty-two-gun frigate *Raleigh*, which was in Boston Harbour. Barry proceeded to Boston and had the *Raleigh* refitted for service and put to sea. The vessel proved unfit for cruising and proceeded to Portsmouth, Virginia, for further refurbishment. On Sunday, 27 September, the *Raleigh* was chased by two British frigates, *Unicorn* and the ship-of-the-line *Experiment*, from nine in the morning to five in the afternoon, and as they neared each other Barry's ship hoisted her colours and one of the frigates hoisted the St George ensign. A broadside from the British ship carried away the foretopmast and mizzentop gallant mast, causing Captain Barry to lose control of the *Raleigh*, much to his grief. The enemy raked the American ship and Barry saw no way of escaping, and with the advice of his officers Barry decided to run his ship ashore on the uninhabited Wooden Ball Island in the rocky Maine inlets.

Commodore John Barry statue on Crescent Quay, Wexford. (Gaul Collection)

On landing, Captain Barry ordered the men to set fire to his ship. An American Midshipman of English origin, one of Barry's crew, quenched the fire, preventing the destruction of the ship. Barry successfully guided eighty-eight of his men to safety, in rowboats to Boston. The entire episode reflected on Barry's concern for the welfare of his crew and his stubborn refusal to surrender. Once again, John Barry was without a ship, although the loss did not lessen his reputation as a skilful commander or mar the character he had won for his bravery.

As his country had no ship to give him, Barry entered the service of his adopted state, Pennsylvania, becoming a privateer and commander of the Letter-of-Marque *Delaware*, a brig owned by Irwin and Company of Philadelphia. He took up this command on 15 February 1779. The *Delaware* was a new brig of 200 tons with ten guns and a crew of forty-five men, which Barry increased to twelve guns and sixty men. On arriving back home from two cruises to Port-au-Prince, Captain Barry was sent immediately to Portsmouth, New Hampshire, where the frigate *America* was on the stocks in the process of building, and where he was to hasten the completion and fitting of the frigate. Barry was replaced by Captain John Paul Jones in overseeing the completion of the *America*, as Barry was doing service at sea in command of the *Alliance*.

Early on the morning of 28 May 1781, an armed ship and a brig were about a league distant from the *Alliance*. At sunup, the ships hoisted the British colours and beat drums. Around eleven o'clock, Captain Barry hailed the ship and was answered that she was a ship-of-war, *Atalanta*, and belonged to His Britannic Majesty. She was under the command of Captain Sampson Edwards. Barry replied that he was commander of the Continental frigate *Alliance*, and advised Edwards to haul down the English colours. Captain Edwards declined, wishing to engage the American ship in battle. Due to lack of wind, the heavier *Alliance* could not manoeuvre quick enough to avoid the gunfire from the *Atalanta* and the *Trepassy*.

Wounded in the left shoulder by canister shot (broken nails, metal fragments and ball shot) while in command of the *Alliance*, Barry remained on deck, bleeding from his many wounds for twenty minutes, until he lost consciousness from loss of blood. He was finally taken below decks for medical care by the ship's surgeon, Mr Kendall. The colours of the *Alliance* were shot, leading the British to think that the American vessel had struck its colours and surrendered. The *Alliance* run up again, and with a rising breeze it was in position to give the *Atalanta* a broadside, and another to the *Trepassy*. Both British ships struck their colours to the *Alliance*. Captain Smith of the *Trepassy* was killed and the captain of the *Atalanta* was brought on board and taken before the wounded Captain Barry in his cabin. The defeated British Captain Edwards advanced and presented his sword to Captain Barry, who returned it to Edwards, saying: 'I return it to you, Sir. You have merited it. Your King ought to give you a better ship. Here is my cabin at your service. Use it as your own.' The crews were taken prisoner and put on board the disarmed *Trepassy*, while the British officers were held as hostages on board the *Alliance*. Barry's ship made sail for Boston with the wounded John Barry.

The last battle of the Revolution took place on 10 March 1783, when the *Alliance* encountered the British frigate *Sybille*, a French vessel captured by the British *Hussar* and now under the command of Captain Vashon. Following his escape from capture, Captain Vashon reported that he had never received such a drubbing as he had from the *Alliance*. On 11 April 1783, Congress ordered by proclamation the cessation of arms by sea and land. On 19 April 1783, Washington announced the end of the war and the disbandment of the army.

France and England engaged in war in 1793, seizing each other's ships on the American coast and sometimes in American waters. A naval force was necessary, and when Congress assembled in December 1793 the main topic for discussion was the building of frigates for the protection of commerce, and from the aggressions of France and from the violation of neutrality by England. Captain John Barry immediately offered his services to his country, and wrote to President Washington on 19 March 1794.[9] A week later, Washington signed an Act declaring that the United States deemed it necessary to form a naval force for its protection. The Act was the foundation for the United States Navy.

Three forty-four-gun frigates and three of lesser tonnage were commissioned. John Barry was appointed captain of one of the ships by the president, which he accepted at once. The commission was not signed or issued by President Washington until 22 February 1797, when the frigate *United States* was ready for launching at Philadelphia. The frigate was built under the supervision of Captain Barry. The County Wexford Irish Catholic boy had become the commander-in-chief of the navy of the new Constitutional United States of America. Barry was appointed by President Washington, 'the Father of his Country' making Barry 'the Father of the American Navy'. His commission reads: 'to take rank from the fourth day of June, one thousand seven hundred and ninety-four'.

In his private life, John Barry married Mary Clary (Cleary) at Old St Joseph's Chapel on 31 October 1767. However, tragedy struck with her premature death at the age of 29 years on 9 February 1774. By this time, Barry's other brothers had made their way across the Atlantic. Patrick was already an experienced mariner, while Thomas embarked on a quieter career as a clerk. Mary died while John was at sea in February 1774, and it was Patrick who was rowed out to his brother's approaching vessel to break the news. Only 29, John Barry found himself a widower.

This sad event was followed some years later by the loss at sea of his brother and fellow mariner, Patrick Barry, in August 1778. His ship, the *Union*, a Letter-of-Marque vessel, sailed from Bordeaux, France, and was never heard from again. Barry married Sarah Keen Austin, Sally to her friends, in July 1777. Sally was an Episcopalian, who eventually converted to Barry's Roman Catholic faith. They had no children of their own but happily reared two boys from John's deceased sister Eleanor's household back in Wexford.

It was a spring day in 1787 when John Barry received word that the *Rising Sun* was very soon to dock in Philadelphia. The ship, under Captain John Rossiter, a friend of Barry's, was returning from a voyage to Wexford. Captain Rossiter, like Barry, was also a Wexford emigrant. Standing on the quay wall awaiting the lowering of the gangplank and the disembarking of the ship's passengers, John Barry and his wife glimpsed Captain Rossiter with two teenage boys. The boys received welcoming embraces from their uncle and a tearful aunt. Michael Hayes, at 18 years of age, was the elder of the two brothers, and the younger brother Patrick was 16 years old. Their sister Eleanor had recently married and remained at home in Ireland.

Following a meal in the town, the Barrys brought Michael and Patrick to their new home at Strawberry Hill. The commodore had 'swallowed the anchor' (a seafaring phrase meaning retirement from sailing), but he encouraged the careers of his nephews. Michael remained with Captain Rossiter on the *Rising Sun* while Patrick set out on a series of voyages free from his uncle's eagle eye.[10]

When the War for Independence ended and the Continental Navy was dissolved, Barry re-entered the maritime trade once more. He sailed to the Orient, bringing back many porcelain and ivory treasures which were eagerly bought by the citizens of Philadelphia. On 22 February 1797, President George Washington gave John Barry Commission Number One in the new Federal Navy. Barry outfitted the first frigates under the Naval Act of 27 March 1794, including his own forty-four-gun USS *United States*, which served as his flagship. He held the courtesy title of commodore. The title 'Father of the Navy' first appeared with the publication of a biographical sketch in Nicholas Biddle's literary journal, *Port Folio*, in 1813. Of the many ships that Barry commanded, the *Alliance* was his favourite and carried his own personal flag, which was of yellow silk with a pine tree and rattlesnake emblazoned on it bearing the motto 'Don't tread on me'. The US Navy has had a battleship named the USS *Barry* in remembrance of this wonderful seaman since those formative years, and it always carries John Barry's flag and motto.

Barry's last day of active service came on 6 March 1801, when he brought the USS *United States* into port. He remained head of the navy until his death on 12 September 1803 from the complications of asthma brought on by the rigours of life at sea. He was buried on 14 September in Old St Mary's Churchyard with full military honours. He was just 58 years of age.

~ 2 ~

YOLA, AN ANCIENT LANGUAGE

Jacob Poole

Jacob Poole (1774–1827), antiquary, son of Josiah Poole and his wife Sarah (daughter of Jacob Martin of Aghfad, Co. Wexford) was born at Growtown, Taghmon, Co. Wexford, 11 February 1774. He was seventh in descent from Thomas and Catherine Poole of Dortrope, Northamptonshire. Their son, Richard Poole, came to Ireland with the parliamentary army in 1649, turned Quaker, was imprisoned for his religion at Wexford and Waterford, and died in Wexford jail, to which he was committed for refusing to pay tithe in 1665.[11]

Jacob's elder brother, Joseph, was born in 1769 and died in 1785. In 1824, Jacob inherited the family estate with extensive land holdings at Growtown and Killianne, where he had lived on family property for some years. Killianne is 4 miles from Wexford town on the Rosslare road. Jacob never lost contact with that area of Wexford and its people, manners, customs and the strange dialect of the Baronies of Forth and Bargy. The inhabitants used to speak an old English dialect, dating from the earliest invasion of the country, and Jacob Poole collected the words and phrases of this expiring language from his tenants and labourers.[12] This collection was edited by the Rev. William Barnes from the original manuscript, and published in 1867 by J. Russell Smith, 36 Soho Square, London as *A Glossary, with some pieces of verse, of the old Dialect of the English Colony in the Baronies of Forth and Bargy*.[13] The glossary contains a total of 1,278 words, noted with great exactitude. The dialect is now extinct, and this glossary also has some fragments of verse. Poole completed the glossary and a further vocabulary or gazetteer of the local proper names in the last five years of his life. It is interesting to note that the glossary has no words beginning with the letter X.

Jacob Poole married Mary, daughter of Thomas and Deborah Sparrow of Holmstown, Co. Wexford, on 13 May 1813, and they had three sons and three daughters.[14] Wherever Jacob went he endeared himself to friends and neighbours because of his unassuming charitable disposition, as the following oft-quoted incident exemplifies. An example of Mr Poole's kindness to his fellow man happened following a visit to William Berry, a respectable Protestant neighbour who resided at Ballykelly, one of Poole's townlands. Berry's wife was a Roman Catholic, whose places of worship were scarce in the Barony Forth. The Roman Catholic community attended a small boxlike shed of mud and timber by the side of the road near the Cross of Killiane known as Amen Cross. It was there, on Sundays and holy days, that a priest celebrated the Holy Sacrifice of the Mass. On a stormy winter day in 1795, while on his return to Growtown to attend on the following day, Sunday, at his own Quaker Meeting House at Forest, Taghmon, he observed a crowd of bare-headed men and kneeling women enduring a strong wind and a clinging mist on the wet and muddy ground. In their midst was his esteemed friend, Mrs Berry. He stopped his horse and returned to his house in Killiane, and next morning visited Fr O'Toole, the local priest. He expressed his concern that his Catholic countrymen were in such a destitute condition to practise their faith, and offered a plot of ground as a gift, free for ever, to use for Catholic worship. By way of a subscription towards the provision of a Catholic chapel, he handed Fr O'Toole ten guinea coins. The Chapel of Kilmachree came into existence soon afterwards in the townland of Ballykelly.[15]

This strange dialect of Forth and Bargy became known as Yola, meaning 'old', and included words and phrases which were a mixture of Irish, Manx and Flemish. Jacob Poole collected and noted these words over a period of time and had hoped to publish this glossary. Richard Stanyhurst (1541–1610), a noted historian, commented on Yola as follows:

Yola only preserved the dregs of ancient Chaucerian English. Yola speakers have so acquainted themselves with the Irish, that they have made a 'gallimaufrere' or 'mingle-mangle' of both languages, so that the natives of Forth and Bargy speak neither good English, nor good Irish.[16]

The leaves of the manuscript are numbered in ink on the recto only as follows: 1, 3, 5, and so on to page 133. The barely legible glossary is written in faded black ink. Poole made various additions and corrections, resulting in a number of very cramped passages. The manuscript was bound by an amateur bookbinder and encased between soft covers. The spine is covered with maroon book cloth, which was trimmed in an uneven manner. There is a title page which contains a list of contents. It is not in Poole's handwriting, and below this, also in a different script, is written:

> Jacob Poole's Glossary of Forth and Bargy Dialect, the only medium through which an effective record of that ancient speech, which died out about 1890, had been preserved. Through my father's medium (his signature below) it was printed in 1867. My father was deeply attached to his uncle Jacob Poole. Overleaf I copy a poem written by my father in 1836, principally referring to this uncle.

This inscription is followed by the name of its writer, A. Webb, and the date 12-7-1908. At the bottom of the title page are the date, 27 August 1866, and the signature and address of Richard D. Webb, 176 Great Brunswick Street, Dublin.[17]

Poole also notes a list of forty-seven surnames common among the inhabitants of the two baronies at that time. The names are written in the Yola spelling and then the English spelling is shown, for example:

> Cuz=zeen - Cousins; Cug=ley - Cogley; Hier=een - Hearn; Preeng=aas - Prendergast; Shoord=aane - Jourdan; Vatte=ean - Fortune; Vur=laune - Furlong; De=roos - Devereux.[18]

Cover drawing from a history of Kilmachree Church.

Kilmachree — in 1780.

Gll ṁA Cṅoɩδe

A selection of Yola words in alphabetical order from over 1,278 listed in Poole's Glossary follows:

Armeen	the side-lace of a car
Baakoozee	to bake bread in an oven
Clugercheen	a flock, clutch or a crowd
Die oaskean	Ash Wednesday
Enteete	a siesta or sleep at noon
Falsakeen	an unprincipled character, a false person
Gendrize	Gentry
Harr	the shank of a button
Joude	a crowd, e.g. Joude an moude or Joude and maude, Crowds and throngs
Khuingoke	a churn
Leeigheen	laughing
Muskawn	a large lump or heap e.g. Muskawn of buthther – a large lump of butter
Nizterels, Niztrols	the nostrils
Oananooree	one another
Paugh-meale	the harvest-home. Paugh-meale seems to be a playful name for the harvest-home, as the kissing time or feast
Quile laaune	a smart lively fellow
Risheen	an afternoon luncheon, a snack in the evening
Sneesheen, Snisheen	snuff
Tharvizeen	scolding
Unket	shy, strange
Vizeen	struggling, contending
Whithel	a sheet e.g. Mucha whithel, a winnowing sheet
Yalpeen	spewing, vomiting
Zin-zetteen	sunset

A short piece of dialogue as recited by Tobias Butler 1823:

Forth dialogue:

A – Aar's a dole o' sneow apa greound to die. Caules will na get to wullaw to-die.

B – Aar's neer a year o aam to be drine-vold.

English translation:

A - There is a deal of snow upon the ground to-day. Horses will not get to wallow (roll) to-day.

B - There is no fear of them to fall into a dry furrow or trench.[19]

'The Bride's Portion', in Forth dialect and an English translation:

A portion ich gae her, was (it's now ich have ee-tolth),
Dhree brailes o' beanes, an a keow at was yole,
A heeve o' been, an dwanty shilleen.

The portion I gave her was (it's now I have told),
Three barrels of beans, and a cow that was old,
A hive of bees, and twenty shillings.[20]

Poole also gives the lyrics of the following songs in Forth dialect with an English translation: 'A Yola Zong'; 'The Weddeen o Ballymore'; 'About an Old Sow Going to be Killed'.[21]

Poole completed the glossary and a further vocabulary or gazetteer of the local proper names in the final five years of his life.[22] Jacob Poole was dogged by rheumatics and repeatedly sought relief while staying with his sister, a resident of 176 Great Brunswick Street, Dublin. She had married into the Webb family, who operated a print company in that area.[23] A poem by Richard Davis Webb, 'The Mountain of Forth', was composed and printed in 1867. Richard was a nephew of Poole and had a great attachment to his uncle. The poem has eleven stanzas, written in rhyming couplets with the sixth couplet refering directly to Richard's uncle:

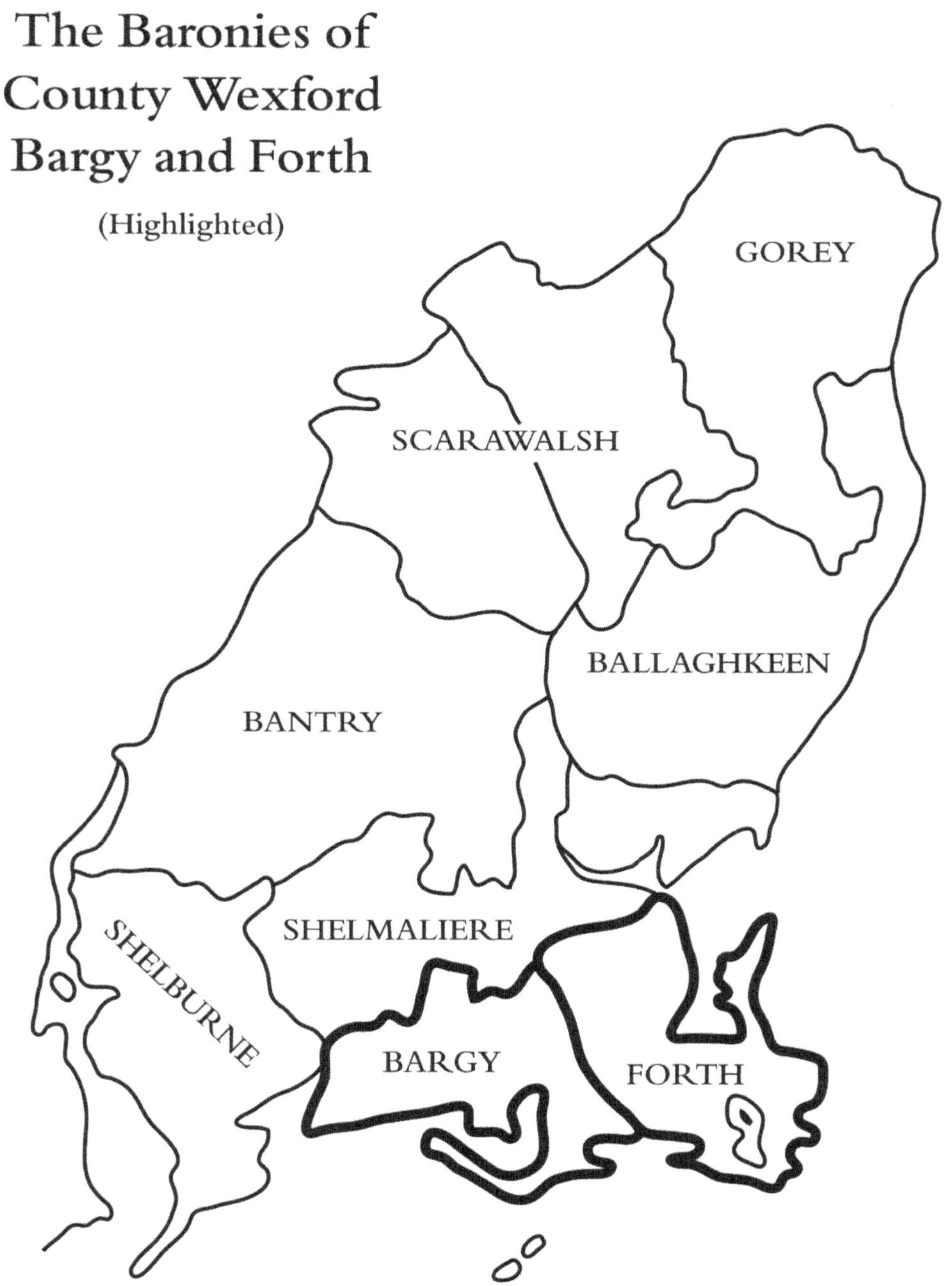

The Baronies of
County Wexford
Bargy and Forth

(Highlighted)

GOREY

SCARAWALSH

BALLAGHKEEN

BANTRY

SHELMALIERE

SHELBURNE

BARGY

FORTH

Map of the Baronies of County Wexford.

His cheerful talk, his frequent sigh, his looks both mild and holy,
His counsel that allured to heaven, and warned from sin and folly.[24]

On becoming less mobile from his disability, Jacob Poole returned to his native Growtown to spend his final years. He died on Tuesday, 20 November 1827 and was buried on the side of a hill in the Burial Ground of Friends in the townland of Forest, Taghmon, County Wexford. The Yola dialect is now extinct, and thanks to the diligence of Jacob Poole the glossary that exists has gone a long way in preserving the remnants of the language for scholars and researchers to explore further. The glossary was published in 1867, forty years following Poole's death and mainly due to the efforts of his nephew Richard Davis Webb. The original manuscript was edited by the Rev. William Barnes and published in London. Even today, in the Baronies of Forth and Bargy a keen ear will detect echoes of a distant past with the usage of some words from the Yola dialect.

— 3 —

POET WITH WEXFORD
CONNECTIONS

Thomas Moore

Songs, poems, Lords and Ladies – and you might think of Thomas Moore, the Poet Laureate of Ireland in the nineteenth century. It was Moore for Ireland and Burns for Scotland. Two eminent poets who captured in their writings and poetry the spirit of their Celtic heritage. The year 1808 marked the publication of Thomas Moore's first volume of his famous *Irish Melodies*. Eight of the twelve airs in the first volume were taken from the Bunting manuscripts.

Thomas Moore's mother, Anastasia Jane Codd, came from Cornmarket and was the daughter of Tomas and Catherine Codd.[25] Following her marriage to John Moore, a Kerry man, who had a grocery and wine business in Dublin, Anastasia maintained strong links with her birthplace in Wexford. Her son Thomas was born on 28 May 1779 at 12 Aungier Street, Dublin. His mother had moved back to Dublin just seven weeks prior to his birth – Moore was almost a true-born Wexfordian. Moore visited Wexford as a boy with family friends, the Redmonds, and met with his grandfather, Tom. He never knew his Wexford grandmother, Catherine, whose maiden name was Joyce, as she had died before Moore was born. He once described Tom Codd as 'my old gouty grandfather'. The Codd household in Cornmarket, which Thomas Moore visited again in 1835, was summed up by him as follows: 'Nothing – could be more humble than the little low house which still remains to tell of his whereabouts.' Moore said that he was never certain of the nature of his grandfather's occupation, although he recalled some weaving machinery in an upstairs room. It seems that Tom Codd would turn his hand to whatever promised a good financial return for his efforts. Anastasia, who was the eldest daughter, benefitted from her father's shrewdness as she brought to her marriage a large dowry.[26] This money enabled her new husband, John Moore, to relocate his business from Johnson's Court to Aungier Street, a more upmarket area of Dublin. The Moores had a large family of eight more children after Thomas's birth, six of whom died young. The other girls who survived were Kate, born in 1782, and Ellen, born four years later in 1786. Anastasia Moore protected her only son and gave him every encouragement to do well at school and any other activity he took to, which included music lessons. Moore returned his love to his dear mother and described her when on one of his visits to Wexford as, 'one of the noblest-minded as well as most warm-hearted of all God's creatures was born under that lowly roof'.

It was while a student at Trinity College that Moore first discovered the collected works of Bunting, just one year following its publication in 1797. Moore credited Edward Bunting with having first made him aware of the 'beauties of our native music'. Thomas Moore was a very competent pianist and together with his friend, Edward Hudson, a flautist, spent many hours playing over the tunes collected by Edward Bunting, the young Belfast organist.[27] Following the successful publication in Edinburgh during the 1790s of Robert Burns' adaptations of Scottish songs, William and James Power, two Dublin music-sellers, thought that they might emulate these publications with a set of Irish songs. They approached Thomas Moore while he was on a visit to his native Dublin in 1806, outlining their idea to him. Moore immediately grasped the possibilities of this idea and contacted John Stevenson, the Irish composer, commissioning him to make piano arrangements for his selected airs. A total of 124 Irish airs were selected and used by Moore and wed to his poetry between the years 1808–34. Eventually, Moore used a total of twenty-six transcriptions from Edward Bunting's massive collection of rich melodic airs. In this first publication of twelve poems and airs, Moore included the poem 'Oh! Breathe Not His Name', which was in tribute to his friend Robert Emmet. The air he used was an O'Carolan composition in praise of 'Doctor John Stafford'.

In the preface to volume one, published on 1 April 1808, Moore stated: 'we have too long neglected the collection of Our National Music'. Praising the wonderful work carried out by Edward Bunting, Moore believed that we had left these treasures of melody unclaimed, with many of our airs being used to enrich operas and sonatas of Continental composers without even an acknowledgement as to their origin.

Above left: Thomas Moore. (Portrait by Martin Shee)

Above right: Anastasia Jane Codd. (Courtesy of the National Gallery of Ireland)

Left: John Moore. (Courtesy of the National Gallery of Ireland)

What did Thomas Moore look like? Moore was a man of short stature, scarcely 5ft tall, with dark curly hair and deep-set eyes and a boyish look which endeared him to all. He won the respect of the most influential people of the time, including Sir Walter Scott; Lord John Russell; editor and poet Leigh Hunt; John Murray, the publisher; Lord Landsdowne; and Lord Byron the poet. Moore was accused of turning his back on his native land and the dying vestiges of Irish culture, yet his poetry and publications of Irish melodies, that otherwise might have been lost, contributed in no small way to their popularity and preservation.

Thomas Moore married Elizabeth (Bessy) Dyke in 1811. She was an actress whom he met while visiting Kilkenny. Thomas and Bessy Moore suffered a lot of private sadness in their married life together, as their five children all died within their lifetimes. They had three daughters – Barbara, Olivia and Anastasia – and two sons, Russell and Tom. Through all of this tragedy, Moore continued to write.

In August 1835, Moore paid a month-long visit to Ireland, which included a trip down the east coast through Wicklow and Wexford, where he was to meet with his friend Thomas Boyse of Bannow. The visit was

Moore in his study at Sloperton. (Courtesy of the National Gallery of Ireland)

all the more joyous as Thomas Moore had just been notified that he was awarded a civil list pension by the new Prime Minister, Lord Melbourne, of £300 per annum. The visit is described in Moore's journal as follows: 'At Gorey, Hume and the others turned back, leaving me to continue on to Enniscorthy by myself. At the inn I met the man who had invited me to the south-east, a wealthy landowner named Thomas Boyse. I found him a pleasant, well-mannered gentle-man.'

In Wexford town he was an honorary local boy. Walking in the Cornmarket, a crowd gathered around him, and led him off to his mother's birthplace. From Wexford, he proceeded with Boyse towards Bannow, on the coast, where a great pageant awaited him. They travelled in style, with rosettes on the horses and cockades in the hats of Boyse's attendants. In the fields, workers paused from the harvest to wave and cheer. A group of outriders carrying green banners met them on the road, and led them back into Bannow. Multitudes now lined the route, chiefly on foot, but also in carriages which joined in the cavalcade. At Boyse's impressive house, The Grange, an arch announced: 'Welcome to Bannow – Welcome Tom Moore.'

The tributes continued as he returned to Wexford town. By special request, he called at the Presentation Convent. He played the convent organ and was then invited to plant a myrtle tree in the garden. After a few days in Dublin, Moore returned to England. There was neither dog nor lion to greet him at Liverpool, but at Alton Towers, where he broke the journey, by invitation of Lord Shrewsbury, he was welcomed by a costumed harpist playing *Melodies* as they arrived. After that, it was Birmingham, Bristol, Bath, and then to his home at Sloperton where he lived for thirty-five years.[28]

The losses of his five children took their toll on Moore's health, and he fell into senile dementia in 1849 and died at his home on 25 February 1852, in his seventy-third year. Moore is buried in the churchyard of St Nicholas' Church at Bromham in Wiltshire. An 18ft Celtic cross marks his tomb with the plinth carrying Moore's own poetic lines:

> Dear Harp of my country in darkness I found thee,
> The cold chain of silence had hung o'er thee long,
> When proudly, my own Island Harp, I unbound thee,
> And gave all thy chords to light, freedom and song.

At Cornmarket in Wexford town, Thomas Moore is also remembered by a plaque set on the facade of the building known today as 'The Thomas Moore Tavern', and bears the following inscription:

IN THIS HOUSE WAS BORN
AND LIVED TO WITHIN A FEW WEEKS
OF THE BIRTH OF HER ILLUSTRIOUS SON

ANASTASIA CODD

THE WIFE OF JOHN MOORE AND MOTHER OF
THE POET

THOMAS MOORE

AND TO THIS HOUSE
ON THE 26 AUGUST 1836, CAME THE POET
IN THE ZENITH OF HIS IMPERISHABLE FAME
TO RENDER HOMAGE TO THE MEMORY
OF THE MOTHER HE VENERATED AND LOVED
THESE ARE HIS WORDS,
'ONE OF THE NOBLEST-MINDED AS WELL AS
MOST WARM-HEARTED OF ALL GOD'S CREATURES
AS BORN UNDER THAT LOWLY ROOF'.

ERECTED DEC. 27TH. 1864
JOHN GREENE, J.P.
MAYOR OF WEXFORD
ERECTED BY THE UÍ CEINNSIALAIGH HISTORICAL SOCIETY
MAY, 15TH 1926,
TO REPLACE ORIGINAL TABLET DAMAGED BY WEATHERING.

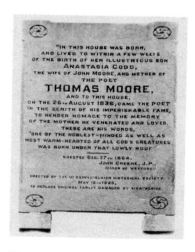

Thomas Moore plaque at Cornmarket,
Wexford. (Gaul Collection)

— 4 —

THE MEN OF '98

Fr John Murphy; John Kelly;
Miles Byrne; Bagenal Harvey

Published historical accounts of the Insurrection of 1798 in County Wexford abound, and give views from both sides, with upheaval involving the Crown forces and the 'local' insurgent forces. The mainly untrained and poorly armed insurgents carrying long-handled pikes, pitchforks and a small amount of firearms faced the well-drilled and highly armed Red Coat soldiers of the king. These were experienced soldiers and cavalry, under the command of officers of high rank who had fought for king and country in many fields of battle. The combined insurgents, both Roman Catholic and Protestant, fought in excess of twenty-one pitched battles across County Wexford at Oulart, Enniscorthy, Gorey, Ross, Wexford, Vinegar Hill, The Three Rocks, Bunclody, Tubberneering, Goff's Bridge, Foulksmills, Ballyellis and into counties Kilkenny, Kildare, Wicklow and Meath. Desecration of places of worship, floggings, pitch-capping, half-hanging and burning of homes were widespread, causing pain and death to the insurgents. Many names have emerged from those turbulent weeks, displaying heroism and valour as they led their men into the jaws of death. Such leading participants in the insurrection were: Anthony Perry, Inch; Esmond Kyne, Mounthoward; Father Michael Murphy, Ballycanew; Edward Fitzgerald , Newpark; George Sparks, Blackwater; John Hay, Ballinkeele; Edward Roche, Garrylough; Thomas Dixon, Castlebridge; Dick Monk, Wexford; William Kearney, Wexford; William Boxwell, Sarshill; William Hughes, Ballytrent; Luke Byrne, Enniscorthy; Father Philip Roche, Poulpeasty; Thomas Cloney, Moneyhore; John Murphy, Loughnageer; and

Walter Devereux, Taghmon. They all held a military rank ranging from general and colonel to captain, and represented the baronies of the county. In a bid to display the heroism and leadership of the insurgent leaders, I have selected just four characters, in brief biographies, who were involved in leading the insurrection, namely: Father John Murphy, a parish curate ministering at Boolavogue Church; Beauchamp Bagenal Harvey of Bargy Castle, a member of the landed gentry; Miles Byrne from Monaseed, who achieved fame in the French army; and John Kelly from Killanne, a young and fearless leader from a prosperous family living in the shadow of Mount Leinster. Their names and deeds are forever emblazoned in the annals of the struggle for freedom during the long, hot summer of 1798.

Rev. Father John Murphy (c.1753–98), a Roman Catholic priest, was one of the leaders of the 1798 Insurrection in County Wexford. Born in the townland of Tincurry, in the Parish of Ferns, he was educated at a hedge school[29] and later at Seville, Spain, where he was ordained to the priesthood in 1785 at the age of 32. He graduated with a Doctor of Divinity degree. On his return to Ireland, he was appointed assistant or curate at Boolavogue in his native county. Originally he was active in promoting loyalty to the government, but when the chapel at Boolavogue was set alight on 27 May 1798, and due to the outrages by the military, Fr Murphy became involved in the insurrection. He took command of the insurgents, and with his army of pikemen he routed the North Cork Militia at the Battle of Oulart and went on to capture the towns of Ferns, Enniscorthy and Wexford.[30] Fr Murphy and his army of pikemen were beaten back by the Crown forces at the Battle of Arklow, County Wicklow, suffering very heavy losses. He joined other insurgent leaders and their pikemen at Vinegar Hill, on the outskirts of Enniscorthy town, where the eleventh battle of the twenty-one in the overall campaign was fought on 21 June. Fr Murphy, together with most of the insurgent armies and their camp followers, made his escape, unharmed, from Vinegar Hill due to a gap left in the ring of steel by the absence of General Needham and his army. Moving on towards County Carlow, Fr Murphy and his companion, James Gallagher, were captured in Tullow on 3 July 1798. Both cleric and layman were publicly flogged in the town square and were hanged and decapitated. Fr John Murphy's body was burned on the rack. His severed head was reportedly brought from Tullow by a Mrs Dawson and was interred in the same grave in Ferns as V. Rev. Andrew Cassin SJ and his nephew V. Rev. Edward Redmond, both parish priests of Ferns.[31]

Beauchamp Bagenal Harvey (1762–98), born at Bargy Castle, County Wexford, was educated at Trinity College, Dublin, and called to the Irish Bar in 1782. Harvey carried on a very successful practice and was known as a supporter of Catholic Emancipation and parliamentary reform. He was a friend of Lord Edward Fitzgerald,[32] Wolfe Tone and other founder members of the United Irishmen, to which he served as president prior to 1793. In conjunction with Anthony Perry of Inch[33] and Edward Fitzgerald of Newpark, he was responsible for the organisation and spread of the United Irishmen in County Wexford. He had previously co-operated with the government in the surrender and collection of weapons in his area of Bargy Castle. On the night of Saturday, 26 May, the eve of the insurrection at Boolavogue, he had travelled to Wexford town to surrender confiscated weapons to the local authorities. Earlier in the day, Anthony Perry signed his confession following torture in which he named the principals in organising an insurrection. On Perry's evidence, Bagnal Harvey was arrested and lodged in Wexford Jail, where he was later joined by Edward Fitzgerald of Newpark and Dr John Henry Colclough, also arrested under suspicion of treachery.[34] Following the Battle of the Three Rocks on Wednesday, 30 May, the Loyalist force evacuated Wexford town and moved south towards Duncannon Fort. The town was now occupied by the insurgents and Bagenal Harvey, Colclough and Fitzgerald were released from jail. Many of the leaders of the rebellion had congregated in the town by evening and established the Wexford Senate, which was established to oversee the government of the county after the insurrection had been successfully concluded. Twelve people from the senate were chosen, divided equally between Protestant and Catholic representatives, to form an executive committee to conduct the affairs of Wexford town and county.[35] Edward Fitzgerald and Dr John Henry Colclough were appointed as colonels to command the insurgent forces, while Bagenal Harvey was commander-in-chief, positions reluctantly accepted by the three men.[36] Harvey tried to bring order out of chaos and restore law and order in the newly formed Wexford Republic.

The Battle of Ross took place on 5 June, commencing at 5.00 a.m., with the insurgents numbering between 10–20,000 men led by Bagenal Harvey. The battle raged until around 4.00 p.m., ending in a defeat for the insurgents, with the loss of more than 3,000 men while the better armed and disciplined military and yeomanry had losses of 200 men.[37] As a result of this massive defeat, Bagenal Harvey resigned as commander-in-chief and was appointed president of the Provisional Council. On Thursday, 21 June, the Battle of Vinegar Hill brought further defeat for the insurgents as the Crown forces captured the nearby town of Enniscorthy, and then advanced under General Moore on Wexford as the last of the insurgents fled the town. Bagenal Harvey and Dr Colclough had returned to their estates, thinking they would be unharmed as they acted under duress in leading the insurgents. They fled to the Great Saltee Island off Kilmore Quay, bringing Dr Colclough's wife with them and a full supply of provisions. They were sought out and their hiding place was discovered, at which point they were arrested and taken back to Wexford town. The captured insurgent leaders were executed in the following days. All of them were hanged, beheaded and their heads placed on the spikes of Wexford Jail.

Arrest of Bagenal Harvey and John Colclough (Cruickshank).

Miles Byrne (1780–1862) was born at Monaseed, County Wexford, on 20 March 1780, the son of a farmer. He joined the United Irishmen in 1797 and played an active role in the Insurrection of 1798. On Sunday, 3 June, he joined a body of insurgents under the command of Fr John Murphy, who had set up camp at Carrigrew. On the same day, General Loftus arrived in Gorey from Dublin with 1,500 troops and five cannon guns. The two insurgent divisions remained at Carrigrew Hill and Carrigbyrne Hill. The next morning, Monday, 4 June, General Loftus left Gorey in a bid to engage with the insurgents at Carrigrew. Loftus divided his force as he headed to Ballycanew and Colonel Walpole was sent to Clogh. Expected reinforcements were to come from Scarawalsh, led by Lord Ancram. At the same time, 10,000 insurgents set out to march on Gorey. The insurgents were armed mainly with pikes, a few muskets with very little ammunition, and no artillery whatsoever. The insurgent army was led by Fathers John Murphy and Michael Murphy, together with Anthony Perry, Edward Fitzgerald, Miles Byrne and Edward Roche. Along the road at Tubberneering the insurgents were opposed by Crown forces under Colonel Walpole, and in the ensuing skirmish Walpole was killed, his troops routed, and his three pieces of artillery with ammunition captured. The town of Gorey was captured and occupied. General Loftus followed the insurgents to Gorey but didn't engage in battle, instead retreating to Carnew, County Wicklow. Loftus and his troops later continued to Tullow, County Carlow. Carnew was deserted by all the loyalists forces.

On Saturday, 9 June, the town of Arklow was attacked by the insurgents. Miles Byrne was in command of a division of pikemen. Arklow had a strong garrison of soldiers under General Needham, and a long battle was contested from 4.00 p.m. until dark, with the eventual withdrawal of the insurgents having suffered heavy losses. The principal insurgent leaders at the Battle of Arklow were Father Michael, who was killed, and Garret Byrne and Miles Byrne.

The Battle of Vinegar Hill took place on 21 June, when the insurgents made their last stand and where Miles Byrne played a distinguished role. Attacked at early dawn by overwhelming columns of troops commanded by General Lake, the insurgents fought with fury, knowing their battles for freedom had ended on this hill overlooking Enniscorthy. Miles Byrne survived Vinegar Hill

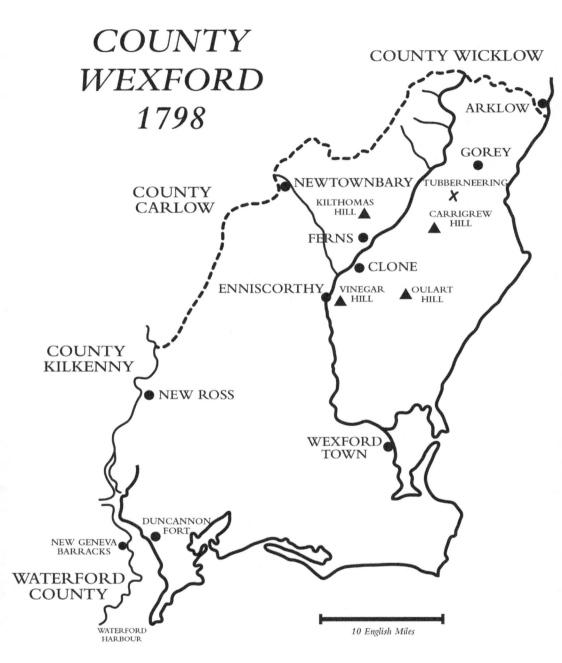

COUNTY
WEXFORD
1798

COUNTY WICKLOW

ARKLOW

GOREY

COUNTY
CARLOW

NEWTOWNBARY   TUBBERNEERING
            KILTHOMAS   X
            HILL ▲   CARRIGREW
                                  HILL ▲
FERNS ●

CLONE ●

ENNISCORTHY   VINEGAR   ▲ OULART
                ▲ HILL   HILL

COUNTY
KILKENNY

● NEW ROSS

WEXFORD
TOWN ●

DUNCANNON
FORT ●

NEW GENEVA ●
BARRACKS

WATERFORD
COUNTY

                    |————————————————|
                    10 English Miles

WATERFORD
HARBOUR

Map of County Wexford, 1798.

and continued the fight in small battles and skirmishes in Counties Wexford, Carlow, Kilkenny, Laois and Wicklow, finally joining with Michael Dwyer and General Holt in the glens of Wicklow. In November 1798, Byrne managed to escape in disguise to Dublin, where for the next few years he worked as a clerk in a timber yard. In 1802–3 he joined with Robert Emmet and other insurgent refugees in Dublin in a bid for another insurrection. The planned insurrection failed, with Emmet fleeing to Rathfarnham. A meeting between Emmet and Byrne resulted in Miles Byrne escaping in an American ship sailing from Dublin to Bordeaux, in a bid to seek assistance from the French government. Miles Byrne travelled to Paris and contacted the refugees there, but soon learned that all hopes of a French intervention were non-existent.

He made the decision to join the French army and served with distinction in Spain, the Low Countries and Germany, continuing in the army after the Restoration, and was appointed *chef-de-bataillon* in 1830. Miles Byrne's *Memoirs,* published in 1863 and edited by his wife, contained many biographical notices and personal details of the Irish exiles in France. He was described by those who knew him in his latter days as a noble-looking old man, erect and soldier-like to the last, with all the polish of a perfect gentleman, genial in his manners and full of anecdotes of various scenes through which he had passed. Miles Byrne, a captain in the Gorey Barony of the insurgent army and a survivor of the Insurrection of 1798, died in Paris on 24 January 1862 in the arms of his beloved wife, aged almost 82 years. He is interred at Montmartre.[38]

John Kelly of Killanne (c.1773–98). The Kelly family originated at Kilbranish near Bunclody, County Wexford. John Kelly's grandfather and family came to reside in Wheelagower c.1760s, where they prospered with a public house, shop and bacon-curing business and as extensive farmers. John Kelly was the first of six children of John Kelly and Mary Redmond, born c.1773. His sisters were Anne, Catherine, Eleanor and a brother, William. A John Kelly's signature appears from time to time in church records from 1779–96 as church warden of St Anne's Church, Killanne. These were laymen appointed to assist in administrative and other duties within the church. The vestry minute books of St Anne's show that a John Kelly attended a vestry meeting on 17 April 1798.

John Kelly enlisted in the United Irishmen in Dublin and was appointed an officer of the Barony of Bantry c.1776. Following the first Battle of Enniscorthy, Kelly arrived at Vinegar Hill, but very soon returned to mobilise the men in his own area to join in the fight for freedom. Kelly was ordered by the commander-in-chief, Bagnal Harvey, to assemble for the attack on Ross. With a company of 800 Bantry men, John Kelly was in situ on the outskirts of Ross, but had orders not to attack the town until two other divisions were in place. On the signal to commence an attack, Kelly and his men swept into the town through the Three Bullet Gate. They immediately went in search of arms to supplement the long-handled pikes they carried. During the onslaught on the town John Kelly was wounded in the thigh and disabled, which was a serious loss to his men for his gallant and fearless leadership. Seriously wounded, John Kelly was taken to Wexford town, to his sister's house in the Cornmarket. He was betrayed and his whereabouts discovered. Kelly was taken from his bed, tried and condemned to death. He was brought to a place of execution on Wexford Bridge where he was hanged, decapitated and his body thrown into the River Slaney. His severed head was displayed on a spike of the courthouse railings with those of Dr John Henry Colclough, Cornelius Grogan of Johnstown Castle, Beauchamp Bagnal Harvey of Bargy Castle and Colonel Matthew Keogh. Colonel John Kelly was 25 years of age.[39]

— 5 —

FOLKLORIST AND AUTHOR
Patrick Kennedy

Patrick Kennedy was born in early 1801 at Kilmyshall, near Bunclody. Little is known concerning his parents or other family members. By the year 1798, there were three or four children in the Kennedy family, with Patrick being either the fourth or fifth child. During the rebellion of 1798, Patrick's mother and her children were a short distance from their house when three mounted yeomen rode up and one of them entered to search the house, and emerged with a lighted sod from the fire. At the point of setting the thatch on fire, one of his compatriots knocked the firebrand from his hand. The three rode away, much to the relief of Mrs Kennedy.[40]

Patrick lived in Kilmyshall until he was 6 years of age, where he received his first education prior to his family living in the Castleboro district. From 1810–14 they lived in the townland of Coolbawn, about 3 miles from Courtnacuddy in the parish of Killegney. When Patrick Kennedy arrived in the parish of Killegney, he went to a school run by a married couple named Bowers. Although they were devout Protestants, their school had Catholic and Protestant children in attendance. Mrs Bowers taught the catechism to the Catholic children without any comment from the local community. In 1813, Patrick went to Shanowel near Taghmon, and resided with relatives of his mother, the Murphy family, reportedly well-to-do farmers. He was to attend a commercial school run by the famous Martin Doyle of Shanowel. He returned to his parents' house after a couple of terms at Shanowel.[41]

In 1814, the Kennedys moved from Coolbawn to the parish of Courtnacuddy, and lived in Beaufield, in the townland of Moneytucker. Later, he continued his education at Cloughbawn, in a school built and supported by the Honourable Robert Carew of Castleboro under the tutelage of Hugh O'Neill. Carew was one of the first landlords in Ireland to build a school for his tenants.[42] Having left school in Cloughbawn, Patrick returned to Kilmyshall to take up a post as a temporary teacher, the substitute for his old school friend O'Brien, who was going to the teachers' training school in Kildare Place, Dublin. When O'Brien qualified he did not return to Tombrick School, leaving Patrick Kennedy in charge of the school. Patrick remained at Tombrick School until he was called to teacher training in 1821. Patrick left Co. Wexford for Dublin, never to return to live permanently. There he trained as a teacher, and was so successful that six months following completion of his training he was recalled to Kildare Place as junior assistant to the superintendant at a salary of £50 per annum with board and lodgings free. He remained there until the Kildare Place Society was dissolved in 1831.[43] He later married Maria Kelly on 24 October 1832. He taught until 1843, abandoning this profession to set up a circulating library and bookshop at the corner of Anglesea and Cope Streets. Kennedy remained in these premises as a bookseller for the next thirty years.[44] His business brought him into contact with many well-known literary and antiquarian figures of the time. He began his writing career when he contributed articles to *The Wexford Independent* under the pen name of Harry Whitney.[45]

Through his literary associations he was encouraged to write about his childhood days in County Wexford, which were eventually published in three books: *Legends of Mount Leinster* (1855), *The Banks of the Boro* (1867) and *Evenings in the Duffry* (1869),[46] all written under his pseudonym of Harry Whitney. *Evenings in the Duffry* has a dedication by Patrick Kennedy, which reads as follows:

To the Revered memory of the Right Honourable the Late Lord Carew. These recollections of a happy period of life spent on the Castleboro Estates, are dedicated by the writer through a deep feeling of respect for his Lordship's indulgent and judicious treatment of his tenantry, as well as a deep feeling of gratitude for many kindnesses received, both a pupil and teacher, in two of the excellent schools established by His Lordship.

The three volumes proved to be extremely popular with readers, but as they were published as cheap paper cover editions the poor quality paper and binding of the books quickly fell apart and disintegrated. Up to recent times these books were only available to peruse in specialist libraries, and have now enjoyed a revival in new printings.[47]

Patrick Kennedy, folklorist and author.

Patrick Kennedy recorded the things he had encountered in his childhood and had retained with great accuracy in his memory. The vanished
world of early nineteenth-century Wexford is described through the words
of its inhabitants in great detail, including the simple enjoyment of fireside chats, where the songs and ballads were sung together with stories of
wakes, mummers and the great escapades of the mighty hurling men on
the playing fields. Although not a great admirer of some of the local ballads,
including the 'Streams of Bunclody', which he described as a 'maudlin lay',
he noted it down nonetheless, preserving it for posterity. This still-popular
ballad was heard by Kennedy at a wake.[48] Tales of historical and patriotic events of the past such as the Whiteboys and the heroes of 1798, the
cattle fairs and faction fights were all recounted by the cheery firesides of
Wexford dwelling houses. Gathered around those hearths the local people
laughed, cried and joked as the various stories were recalled, and the 'characters' that abounded in the village were brought to life, from the faggot
cutter to the gentleman farmer, the parish priests, the blacksmith and the
hedge school master.[49]

In his preface to *The Fireside Stories of Ireland*, published in 1870, Patrick
Kennedy declares that in this volume of stories he had intended to include
some Ossianic and saintly legends and short historic romances from Ireland's
ancient annals, but decided that such tales could await another publication to
make their appearance in print. He explains that the greater number of the
stories in this 'new' collection had previously been published in the *Dublin
University Magazine*, which was owned by Joseph Sheridan Le Fanu, and to
whom he expressed his gratitude for the kind permission granted to repub-
lish the stories in a separate edition. As a folklorist, Patrick Kennedy hoped
that his present collection might give pleasure to many a young unsophisti-
cated reader, and revive healthy and pleasant recollections of early life in the
hearts and minds of those advanced in years.

For many years, prior to his first book being published in 1855, Kennedy
had been writing and submitting articles and reviews to the *Wexford
Independent* and Duffy's *Fireside Magazine* and other periodicals of interest to
folklorists. It was Sheridan Le Fanu[50] who first convinced Patrick Kennedy
that his writings should be put into book form. In his dedication to Le Fanu

in *The Legendary Fictions of the Irish Celts*, Kennedy states that his stories would never have appeared in book form but for Le Fanu's encouragement. The collected writings of Kennedy formed the nucleus of the books that were to follow. It was his main objective to preserve the traditions of his native county, and in a letter to the editor of the *Wexford Independent* newspaper he requested its readers to send him any outline of local traditions, which he would later include in the *Whitney Papers* especially for the benefit of the young folk.[51]

A short few weeks following Le Fanu's persuading Patrick Kennedy to have his stories published, Kennedy died on 29 March 1873 in his seventy-second year, and is buried in Glasnevin Cemetery, Dublin. The humble and self-effacing bookseller of Cope and Anglesea Streets left a treasure house of Wexford folklore in his writings. Possibly regarded as a pioneer in this field of research and preservation, albeit by simple methods, he was the precursor of Jeremiah Curtin,[52] Douglas Hyde[53] and James Hamilton Delargy,[54] the eminent gentlemen who were responsible for setting up the Irish Folklore Commission.

— 6 —

WEXFORD CHURCH BUILDER

Fr James Roche

ECCE SACREDOS MAGNUS
(BEHOLD THE GREAT PRIEST)

Down the centuries of her chequered history, the town of Wexford has borne many famous sons, men who made their mark in every walk of life in Church and State, on land and sea, in music and art as well as commerce. Yet who would question the claim of Father James Roche to be called 'the greatest of them all'. Never had a town a more loyal and devoted son, or one who was prouder to call himself by the honoured name of 'Wexfordman'. As a priest of God and pastor of Wexford, he was heir to an ecclesiastical tradition that had '*Pro Deo et Pro Patria*' (For God and Fatherland) for its motto, but who can look at the beautiful twin churches of Wexford town and not feel that in the heart of Father Roche was engraved an even more personal dedication: 'For Our Lady and my Native Town'.

Father James Roche was a Wexfordman, born and reared in a house at the corner of South Main Street and Oyster Lane, where his parents ran a provision merchants and public house. In the parish register we find the date of his birth as 21 August 1801.[55] As a small boy of 6 or 7 years he went, like the sons of many of the merchant class of his day, to the school in George Street, Wexford, conducted by the Rev. Mr Behan, a Protestant gentleman. Here he had as fellow pupils the Devereux brothers, Richard and Thomas, who in later years, as Catholic laymen, were to have their names enshrined on the history of Wexford parish. All three being of noble and generous disposition, they soon formed a friendship that was to last as long as life itself.

In 1811, James Roche, now nearly 10 years of age and already feeling the first promptings of priestly vocation, entered the diocesan seminary which had just been opened at Michael Street, Wexford under the presidency of Dr Myles Murphy.[56] He continued his studies here until the establishment was closed down on the opening of the new St Peter's College at Summerhill in 1819.[57] He did not, however, become a student of St Peter's, for in the autumn of that same year he began his ecclesiastical studies at St Patrick's College, Maynooth, Co. Kildare.

Fr Roche was ordained on Pentecost Sunday, 1826, and began his missionary career as a curate in Enniscorthy, Co. Wexford, where he was appointed in the spring of 1827. He laboured in Enniscorthy for thirteen years, becoming administrator in 1830. During this period, party spirit and sectarian bitterness had led to much strife and unhappiness in the town, but Father Roche, with great zeal and diplomacy, poured oil on the troubled waters and by precept and example enforced the Divine Law of Brotherly Love.[58]

In 1840, on the death of the Rev. William O'Neill, Father Roche was appointed parish priest of Ferns, Co. Wexford, where he found the new church, begun by his predecessor, still unfinished and heavily burdened with debt. In a few years he had completed the church and gone a long way towards clearing off the debt as well. About this time, also, the man who was already making a name for himself as a 'church builder' found time for pursuits of a different nature. He turned for a while to study the history of his parish. The result of his endeavours in this field was a *Life of St Aidan*, first bishop and patron of the diocese of Ferns. As a literary composition and historical record it was, to use the language of that time, 'greatly esteemed by the cognoscenti of all professing Christians'.

St Aidan, detail from Harry Clarke window, 1919.

On 25 June 1850, following the death of Rev. Dr Sinnott, P.P., Father Roche was transferred to the parish of Wexford.[59] In January of that year a meeting had been held at which it was decided to build two new churches in the town. Proof of Father Roche's organising ability is found in the fact that the foundation stones of both churches were laid on 27 June in the following year. The building, furnishing and financing of these churches was to be the main object of his zeal and energy for the next thirty years. Both churches were designed by Richard Pierce, an architect from Tenacre, County Wexford. Pierce had learned his architectural skills from the Gothic architect Augustus Welby Pugin.[60]

In April 1854, the zealous pastor found time to visit Rome and have a private audience with the then Holy Father, Pius IX, from whom he personally received the Apostolic Blessing for himself, his parishioners and all who should give donations towards the completion of the new parochial churches of Wexford. He paid a second visit to the Holy City in 1862.

It is no exaggeration to say that as the result of his church-building activities, combined with great personal charm, Father Roche became, in his day, the best known and most respected figure in the town. He knew his people both rich and poor, nor were the strangers, even passing ones, allowed to remain long outside the circle of his friendship. On the death of Dr Furlong in 1875, the chapter of the diocese did Canon Roche the honour of electing him to the office of vicar capitular, to administer the affairs of the Church during the vacancy of the episcopal see.

In May of the following year, the parishioners found an opportunity to show their loyalty and appreciation of their pastor's worth. It was the fiftieth anniversary of his ordination to the priesthood. To mark the event, a great meeting was held in the Town Hall in Wexford and the beloved canon was presented with an Address of Congratulation, in which he was acclaimed as 'a distinguished and exemplary Priest, a credit to the Church of God, and a man of whom his native town had just reason to be proud'. On this occasion the *Te Deum* was sung in the parish churches and in the chapels of all the religious communities in the town.

Having built and furnished the twin churches and having completely organised religion in the parish, Canon Roche might justifiably enough

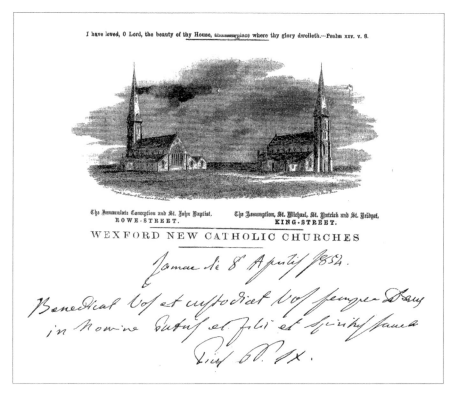

I have loved, O Lord, the beauty of thy House, and the place where thy glory dwelleth.—Psalm xxv. v. 8.

The Immaculate Conception and St. John Baptist.
ROWE-STREET.

The Assumption, St. Michael, St. Patrick and St. Bridget,
KING-STREET.

WEXFORD NEW CATHOLIC CHURCHES

Apostolic Benediction from Pope Pius IX, 1854.

have taken things more easily during the latter years of his life. The cost of this massive project was £54,000, with monies contributed and collected from all possible sources to finance the building. Each month a list was published in the local newspapers with names and amounts subscribed. Protestant donations were prominent among the offerings. Everyone was called upon to raise the necessary funds, from the labouring family to the gentry. Wexford was a great maritime port, and when Wexford owned ships docked at the quayside they were expected to contribute their share, and the sailors dared not go into the local taverns until they had first made their contribution to Fr Roche's fund. A Quaker gentleman with a retail outlet in the town once turned down the canon's request for a contribution, saying, 'Me and mine have nothing to do with thee and thine and I will give thee nothing.' Fr Roche replied, 'If me and mine had nothing to do with thee and thine, then thee might as well close up shop.' The Quaker so admired Fr Roche's reply that he made an admirable contribution to the fund.[61] Even the building of the churches must not be allowed to eclipse the other splendid achievements in a lifetime of surpassing zeal, including the opening of the Christian Brothers' School in George Street, Wexford, bringing the Loreto nuns to Richmond House in 1866, the founding of the Order of Perpetual Adoration at their first convent at Rock-Field in 1868 and establishing of the Sisters of St John of God in 1871. The building of the Christian Brothers' Monastery and Schools, in Joseph Street, was completed in 1875.

Fr Roche was the last parish priest of Wexford. The parish became mensal, the bishop's parish, and from that time to the present day it is run by an administrator. He died at his residence, St Aidan's, Waterloo Road, on Wednesday morning, 14 March 1883. He had been ailing for several months and for some weeks had been confined to his room. During the last few days, the constant companions at his bedside were his brothers, Father John Roche, OFM of the Franciscan Friary, Wexford, and Father Thomas Roche, PP of Our Lady's Island, who said Mass each morning in the little oratory at St Aidan's and brought Holy Viaticum to the dying pastor. As the crowning joy of a life spent so unselfishly in the service of God, Canon Roche had the privilege of being able to receive his master for the last time just a few moments before he died. '*Beati Mortui qui in Domino Moriuntur*' (Blessed are the dead who die in the Lord). On Thursday evening at four o'clock, the remains were given a public funeral from St Aidan's, Waterloo Road to the Church of the Immaculate Conception, the route being along John Street, Hill Street, The Quay, William Street, Maudlintown, the Faythe, Castle Street, Main Street, George Street, John Street and back to the church, where the body lay in state until Friday morning. After Requiem Office and High Mass, the remains were removed to the Church of the Assumption to be interred in front of Our Lady's Altar, which is not more than 100 yards from the spot in South Main Street where Father Roche was born. Four years following his death, a statue of this great priest was erected in the grounds of the Church of the Immaculate Conception, Rowe Street, designed by Sir Thomas Farrell. One of the local streets and a terrace of houses situated between the two churches were named in honour of Canon James Roche. These two magnificent Wexford churches remain as the legacy of Fr James Roche to his native town.[62]

— 7 —

ARCTIC EXPLORER
Sir Robert John Le Mesurier McClure

It was Wexfordman, Robert John Le Mesurier McClure, who made the discovery of the Northwest Passage in 1853. He was the only son of Captain Robert McClure and Jane Elgee. Captain McClure was an army officer with the 89th Regiment, Princess Victoria's Royal Irish Fusiliers.[63] Jane's father was the Rev. John Elgee, a Church of Ireland curate in Wexford in 1790. He married Jane Waddy, daughter of Cadwalladar Waddy, owner of several properties in the town.[64] Following the death of his wife, Rev. Elgee was appointed Archdeacon of Leighlin in 1804[65] and moved to the Glebe House in the Bullring, while Jane and her husband Robert took up residence in her father's home on Foreshore Street. Their son, Robert, was born on 28 January 1807, five months after his father died in 1806.[66] Robert John Le Mesurier McClure was baptised on 30 January, as recorded in the parish register at the Church of Castlebridge, County Wexford.

On reaching 4 years of age, Robert McClure was placed into the care of his godfather, General John le Mesurier, the last hereditary Governor of Alderney in the Channel Islands. Robert lived there until 1819, before entering Eton and then Sandhurst Military College, which he disliked, and at 16 years of age he joined the navy. He began his naval career on board HMS *Victory* and over the coming twelve years served in different parts of the world, culminating in a promotion to lieutenant in 1830. An invitation in 1836 from Sir Charles Adams to join an expedition preparing for a voyage to the North Pole was accepted by McClure. He was appointed to the *Terror* under the command of Captain George Back, bound for Repulse Bay. Leaving Chatham on 14 June, the vessel crossed Davis Strait on 28 July 1836. Navigation through massive ice floes gave McClure first-hand experience of the dangers involved in such treacherous conditions. The expedition returned to England by the end of 1837. He then signed on as first lieutenant of the *Investigator* with Captain Bird, travelling to the Arctic as part of an expedition led by Sir James Clark Ross in 1848.[67]

Under the command of Captain Richard Collinson, CB, senior officer and leader of the expedition to the *Enterprise*, and Commander Robert Le Mesurier McClure to the *Investigator*, the two ships set sail from the River Thames on 10 January for Plymouth, for the caulking of both vessels. Fully prepared for a six-month sailing, the Arctic Squadron weighed anchor on 20 January 1850 in an attempt to find the Northwest Passage between the Pacific and Atlantic Oceans.[68] This expedition was the nineteenth such venture, stretching over 400 years previously.[69] The *Investigator* was 400 tons, registered and purchased from Messrs. Green of Blackwall.[70] The ship also carried water and meat casks, sledges, ice-triangles, ice-saws and a crow's nest. Including McClure, the ship carried officers and crew of sixty-five, with a surgeon, carpenters, sail maker and even a blacksmith.[71] Captain McClure also brought an interpreter – a German, Mr Mierching – as part of his crew. McClure described his crew as, 'a more orderly set of men have seldom been collected'. Throughout the voyage his crew battled with foul weather, strong winds and heavy seas.

On 18 March, the *Investigator* crossed the Southern Tropic in the Atlantic Ocean, and a month later on 17 April the *Investigator* reached the Chilean penal settlement at Port Famine and sailed onward to Hawaii. By this time, the *Investigator* had completed a sea voyage of 15,000 miles, and having stocked up again with extra provisions, left Honolulu bound for the Arctic voyage. The ship crossed the Arctic Circle on 29 July 1850, and the weather changed so dramatically that the crew were issued with clothing suitable for these conditions. A few days later, on the morning of 2 August, the first ice was seen ahead with large herds of walruses basking on the loose ice masses. The *Investigator* was off the Wainwright Inlet on 5 August, and made rapid progress to Point Barrow, entering the Arctic Ocean from Behring's Straits and leaving the Pacific Ocean behind them. When close to the shore at Point Pitt, the master, Mr Court, was sent ashore to erect a marker cairn of stones. There they met with the first Inuit people, who referred to the visitors as *kabloonas*.[72] A friendly communication was established with Mr Court through the ship's interpreter, Mr Mierching. As a token of friendship, the *Investigator* gave away knives and mirrors to the Inuit people. Tobacco was a great favourite with the Esquinmaux and was much requested from the ship's crew. The name of McClure's ship was engraved on the items, ensuring that those who might communicate with the natives would know that the named ship had come this distance. The *Investigator* made good progress through the ice and passed Flaxman's Island on 18 August, and on the following day ice of enormous thickness and in large and extensive floes some 7 to 8 miles long was on either side of McClure's ship. Fearful of being trapped and crushed between the ice floes, McClure turned his ship southward, sailing against a freshening wind. On 20 August, the Buckland Mountains came into view as McClure sailed clear of the ice.

The next day, 21 August, the sea was clear of ice and the ship steered off the Pelly Islands, and a week later the *Investigator* sailed from Cape Warren to Port Dalhousie. Now perpetual daylight was giving way to three hours of total darkness, so the *Investigator* fired guns and rockets at intervals, hoping that some of Franklin's expedition or the *Enterprise* might be near. By the end of August, having crossed Liverpool Bay, the ship reached Cape Bathurst and sailed round the bay formed by Capes Bathurst and Parry, where pods of whales were sighted. On 5 September, fires were seen and McClure, thinking it was the Inuit, dispatched Lieutenant Gurney Cresswell, Dr Armstrong and others to check. The fires were volcanic, coming from fifteen holes in the ice. Specimens of earths and minerals were collected by Dr Armstrong. On the following day the expeditionary ship reached Cape Parry, and the following day Captain McClure landed to take possession of this addition to the realms of Queen Victoria and named the land 'Baring Island', in honour of the First Lord of the Admiralty, Sir Francis Baring.

With the ice floes closing in, the *Investigator* was thrown over to the starboard side and lifted 2ft out of the water as the ice pressed under the keel. The ship's timbers cracked and groaned and the ship's bells began to ring as the vessel surged and trembled with the shock. The *Investigator* was locked solid in the ice. To break the monotony, part of the lower deck was converted in the evenings into a temporary stage, where some of the crew performed, danced, sang and recited for the amusement of the rest of the crew. Stocks of food were constantly checked, and at

Sir Robert John Le Mesurier McClure portrait.

one stage 500lb of canned meat were declared putrid as the tins had been damaged when being stowed prior to leaving England – all the meat had to be thrown overboard. On 21 October 1850, Captain McClure set out by sledge with a party of six men, commanded by Mr Court, for Barrow's Strait, leaving the ship in charge of Lieutenant Haswell. With the repeated capsizing of their sledge it was damaged beyond repair, so McClure sent Mr Court back to his ship for another sledge. The remainder of the group pitched the tent and slept under canvas on the frozen ocean. The following days were hazardous and demanding, as the men pulled their new sledge over the frozen ridges of snow and ice. The party were disappointed they had not sighted Barrow Strait on the 25th, yet they felt excited by the many proofs around them of being close.

The morning of 26 October 1850 was fine with a clear sky overhead, so Captain McClure and his men set out before sunrise to climb a nearby hill and ascended to 600ft above sea level. They waited for the daylight to increase, in the hope of seeing the long sought-for Northwest Passage. The rising sun slowly revealed a panorama showing Prince Albert Land to the

east, and from a point named for Sir Robert Peel turned to the east forming the northern entrance of the channel on that side. The coasts of Banks
Island stretched to about 12 miles from where the expeditionary party were
standing. At the height of 600ft the eye had a better view of seeing any land
between them and Melville Island, formerly called Barrow's. The Northwest
Passage had been discovered.[73]

All the long-held doubts of such a link between the two oceans had
been removed, and the feelings of Captain McClure and his men considering all they had gone through to make this discovery. In an effort to
navigate around Banks Island in 1851, McClure reached the Bay of Mercy,
where he wintered. A sledge party reached Melville Island and back, and
left a message in Winter Harbour. By the spring of 1852, the crew were
malnourished and on the brink of death. Help arrived with Lieutenant
Bedford Pim, who walked around the ice to the *Investigator*. He was keen
to sail his ship back to England, but was ordered to abandon it. McClure
and crew spent the winter of 1853 in the Arctic, and in April 1854 he went
by sledge to Beechey Island, where he sailed back to England on the *North
Star*. He was court-martialled for the loss of his ship, and was acquitted and
awarded £10,000 to share with his men.[74] Captain Robert McClure was
knighted and later made an admiral, and wrote an account of his Arctic
expeditions in *Voyages*.

In a letter to Alderman Greene, proprietor of the *Wexford Independent*,
Richard Waddy Elgee, Rector of Wexford wrote:

The Rectory, Wexford

21 October 1853

Dear Sir – Perceiving by the public papers, that misapprehension prevails
as to the birth-place of Captain McClure, I beg to state that he was born
at No. 105 North Main Street, in this town, the residence at that time
of his maternal grandfather, the late Venerable Archdeacon Elgee, Rector
of Wexford; and that I had the pleasure of seeing him on the day of his
birth. Requesting that you will have the kindness to give a place to this
communication in your valuable paper, I remain, dear Sir, your faithful
servant. [75]

At a special assembly at the Spring Assizes 1855 of the Grand Jury of the County of Wexford, a toast was paid to Sir Robert McClure when the chairman addressed the assembly as follows:

> Fill your glasses, gentlemen. allow me another favour, that of calling on Mr. George LeHunte[76] to propose the next toast.
>
> We are met to honour the brave, and the toast I am about to propose is that of not only a brave man, but of a man born in the town of Wexford, 'Captain Robert McClure, our noble fellow townsman, the discoverer of the North-West Passage'. England had seriously engaged in the question, a rivalry arose with other nations, and to England has fallen the palm and the prize, but it was a Wexfordman achieved the victory. Gentlemen, I have the honour to propose the health of Captain Robert McClure.[77]

Sir Robert married Ada, daughter of Mr Richard H. Tudor of Birkenhead, in 1867. His death occurred on 17 October 1873, aged 66 years. He was buried at Kensal Green Cemetery on 25 October.[78]

Sketch by Lt Samuel G. Cresswell (1827–1867) of HMS *Investigator* marooned in pack ice.

~ 8 ~

THE IRONMASTERS

James Pierce and Sons

One of County Wexford's most famous sons was an inventor, businessman and founder of Ireland's foremost agricultural engineering company, Philip Pierce & Co., also known as Mill Road Ironworks in Wexford town. The founder, James, was eventually succeeded by his sons, Philip, Martin, James and John.

Born in Kilmore village, County Wexford, James Pierce's baptism was recorded in the parish register as 13 August 1813. His parents were Philip Pierce and Mary Connor.[79]

The Pierce family lived in a small thatched cottage located near the present entrance to the priest's house. It was easy to find the Pierce household, as the front area of the house was paved in black stones showing the initials P.P. (Philip Pierce) painted in white. Philip Pierce had a forge on the opposite side of the road where it is likely the young James Pierce worked with his father as a blacksmith. This is a point which has often been disputed, for it was said that James served as a millwright, engaged in building windmills around Wexford and as far afield as Kilkenny. On the decline of the blacksmithing business c.1830, James Pierce set his sights on emigrating to Argentina, but a change of mind brought him into Wexford town where he established a small engineering works in Anne Street, a short distance from the busy quayside. He was possessed of an inventive brain and quickly realised the rapid and revolutionary changes happening in all aspects of agricultural engineering.[80]

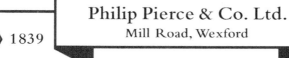

Philip Pierce & Co. Ltd.
Mill Road, Wexford
1839   1965

James Pierce

Philip Pierce

Martin Pierce

John Pierce

Philip B. Pierce

Agricultural Machinery Manufactured in Wexford

Philip Pierce & Co. Ltd – the family.

One of Pierce's first inventions was the 'Fire Machine', becoming widely known as the Pierce fire fan. This fire fan proved to be revolutionary, especially for the farmer's wife and cottage dwellers, when a few turns of the fire fan quickly sent flames shooting up the chimney as the fire was rekindled. This relatively simple invention by James Pierce soon proved to be popular, not only in Ireland, but was also to be found in many an elegant pile in neighbouring Britain. The fire fan was in use for many years until its gradual decline following the invention of the new stoves and modern cookers. The crane and hooks in the open fireplace faded into the past.

James Pierce went on to develop new inventions, most notably the horse threshing machine in 1846 and several other horse machines. Business expanded to such a degree that he was obliged to transfer to a more spacious site in Allen Street, Wexford. Some of his more notable works outside the farm machinery field were the manufacture and erection of the railings around the twin churches in Wexford, the erection of a conservatory for Sir James Power at Edermine House, and making the first printing press for *The People* newspaper in 1853. One account I came across states that James Pierce got his first big break when an English warship was wrecked on the south coast of Wexford. The vessel contained a large number of heavy guns, and Pierce entered into a contract to remove them and bring them the 14 miles by road to Wexford. He did this by fitting wheels and axles to the cannons.[81] As his business continued to grow, he acquired what was to become the permanent home for his works at the Folly, where previously there was a corn mill driven by water power and owned by Thomas Reville, whose family belonged to the Lough, Duncormick. In 1856, James Pierce secured a contract to erect a bridge over the River Slaney at Carcur, Wexford. At this point the river is a quarter of a mile in width from bank to bank. The currents at this point are particularly strong, and in addition the bed of the river is of soft sand, with continuous movement.[82] The bridge was designed by Thomas Willis, to the plans of James Barry Farrell. This bridge was in use until 1959.[83] In 1866, the eldest son, Philip, joined his father in the management of the expanding company, and when James died in December 1868, Philip took over. James was only 56 when he died of pneumonia.

His death notice in *The People* described him as 'a gentleman whose mechanical genius was of the highest order and whose good heart and gentle temper won the regard of all who knew him'. The *Wexford Independent*, on the other hand, noted that he was highly respected 'but was not trained in the top social graces'.[84] He was buried in the Franciscan cemetery in Wexford. Philip lived at Rocklands House, possessed all of his father's inventive and commercial genius, and under his guidance, later joined by his brother Martin, the firm prospered at an amazing pace, establishing exports to all parts of the globe including Australia, Asia, Central and South America as well as England, Scotland and Wales.

At the end of June 1884, George Bassett first visited the firm of Philip Pierce & Company, where he was given a tour of the works by Mr Philip Pierce whom, with his brother Martin, made up the active management. Bassett goes on to note, for the sake of his readers, a very good description of the foundry, and I quote from Bassett:

I had better mention that the leading manufacturers of Messrs. Philip Pierce & Co., are mowers, reapers, horse power and steam power threshing machines, churning machines, horse rakes and turnip and mangold seed sowers. As the principal parts of such machinery take shape primarily at the foundry, I began to make notes there. The building which enclose it are 56 by 100 feet. They are constructed of stone and have brick facings. Three years ago those buildings were made two-thirds larger. The most improved moulding machinery, fitted for steam power, is used and there are two blast furnaces of very considerable capacity.

Original Fire Blower (Fire Fan).

Next in order to the foundry is the fettling shed. Here the castings are taken in the rough and placed for the purpose of cleaning in a revolving cylinder after which they are trimmed by emery wheels driven by steam. From the fettling shed the castings are removed to a large store, capable of holding 150 tons. Each kind is carefully placed by itself so that at a glance it may be seen where renewal of stock is most needed. An idea of the number of castings required for the successful operation of such a factory as that of Messrs. Philip Pierce & Co., may be formed when I mention that in this store there were from 600 to 700 varieties.

Following in the regular order of progress toward the completion of the perfect machine, an uncovered space of several hundred feet had to be passed between the castings store and the fitting shop. This was nearly all occupied with piles of the larger castings, including thousands of moving machine wheels.

The turnery is the most interesting part of the works. Here are the contrivances of mechanical ingenuity which shape the products of the foundry to the exact sizes required for accurate machine building. It is about 150 feet in length and has nine sliding lathes, six vertical and horizontal drilling machines, slotting and recessing machines and punching and shearing machines. Over 200 pulleys were in motion and certainly not less than 2,000 feet of belting. It took only a casual glance to understand that no expense had been spared in the equipment and I was not at all unprepared to hear from Mr. Pierce that many valuable improvements in the machinery had been made by himself.

In the erecting shop, which is 80 by 120 feet, the various parts of the machines are put together. A tramway runs from the erecting shop to the machine store, which is 60 by 120 feet and is large enough to easily hold from 500 to 600 mowing machines and 200 threshing machines. In this house there was ample evidence of good taste in finish and of durability in construction of the various machines. Next to the machine store is the iron store, a building of 80 by 40 feet. It was arranged, with the precision noticeable in every other department, the immense stock of bar, scrap and pig iron necessary for the supply of such extensive operations. The working rules of the factory are displayed for all to observe and which apply to all workmen. The hours of labour are from six to six, from Monday to Friday and on Saturday from six o'clock to three.

The grounds belong to the Mill Road Iron Works consist of four and a half acres and these are largely covered by buildings. One of the open spaces seen from a distance is so occupied by horse-rakes as to suggest a regiment of soldiers with fixed bayonets. Not the least important of the divisions of the concerns, which are so admirably calculated, is the part store. This is 80 by 25 feet, and has sections of bins running from floor to ceiling, in which are kept the wearing parts of machines. During the last six years the development of this industry as a whole necessitated an outlay of between £4,000 and £5,000 on new buildings, among which are handsome offices.[85]

From the company's agency office in Paris and South America came the names of the Pierce-built houses in Wexford – Avenue de Flandres and Casa Rio. A big blow came in 1895, when Philip Pierce, after whom the company was named, died at the young age of 49 from pneumonia. He was unmarried and was buried with his father in the friary cemetery. Strangely, they are not included in the records made of the burials there before the headstones were removed.

Martin, living at Park House, was then left in control, but he also tragically died at the same age (49) as a result of being stranded on the Saltee Island following a boating mishap in 1907. He owned the island at the time, and frequently visited it. It was he who introduced the Pierce bicycle, which was discontinued after some years. Martin was buried in Crosstown cemetery with his wife Mary, who had died the previous year.

In 1910, there was a major fire in the factory which resulted in a rebuilding and extending of the work premises. The onset of the First World War in 1914 created many problems for the foundry, as their overseas markets were lost and iron was in short supply. Sales of machinery on the home market were also restricted. However, the war did create some work from the government in the manufacture of shell cases for the war effort. Cast steel was also in such short supply that to keep their mowing machines operational, Pierce's manufactured machine 'fingers' from bronze.[86]

The furnace men 'tapping' out metal from one of the four cupolas.

The reins of control then passed to the youngest son, John, who had been an official with the Provincial Bank in Cork. He changed his religion when he married Susan Busteed, daughter of a Protestant farmer. There were about 1,000 men employed when he took over the firm and he steered it through the difficult period of the First World War, which dealt a great blow to the company's export market. John Pierce died while on business in Paris in 1926, and was buried there. John was father of the late Philip B. Pierce, and his twin sister Ethel Geraldine. She married Jim Harvey of Bargy Castle and died in London in 1981, and is buried with her mother, Susan, in Crosstown. Philip B. Pierce was serving in the British Army at the time of his father's death and was brought home to take over the company, which he headed for over three decades. He inaugurated the highly successful edge tool factory in 1928 and saw the Pierce plough win national prominence in county and All-Ireland ploughing championships in the 1930s. Though he began life in the Protestant faith of his parents, and attended services and Sunday school in St Selskars, Philip B. Pierce became an ardent Catholic through the influence of his pious maiden aunts who lived in Rocklands House. Like his grandfather, James, and uncle, Philip, he became very attached to the Fransciscan friary. However, in later life he changed his patronage to Barntown Church. When Philip B. Pierce died suddenly at his home in Dublin in 1979, aged 85, he was buried with his mother in the Protestant section of Crosstown Cemetery, but was reinterred the following year with his uncle Martin in the Catholic section nearby.[87]

The last of the Pierce sisters lived in Rocklands House: Alice, who died in 1934, and Anne in 1935. Alice was a talented artist and painted many beautiful pictures. The eldest of James Pierce's family, Joanna, died unmarried in 1918. I have been unable to trace what became of the other sisters, Mary and Catherine, one of whom, I am told, entered a convent. Neither have I been able to trace what became of James junior, born in 1859. He may have died young.[88]

When Philip B. Pierce married Nancy O'Brien from St John's Road, Wexford and lived in Park House, his mother, Susan, moved out of Park House to Killingney, Summerhill, where she resided until her death in March 1944. She requested a private funeral and no mourning. Philip Pierce carried out elaborate innovations to the grounds of Park House, which he opened to the public. They had three children: Perpetua Anne Mary, who is called Pam; Philipa Jacinta; and one son who was appropriately named Philip.

One hundred and twenty years after the foundation of the company by James Pierce, the foundry changed hands in 1964 when it was bought, together with its main rival, the Wexford Engineering Company, by the Smith Group. The Star Ironworks formerly operated by the Wexford Engineering Company was closed while the foundry and edge tool plant was carried on by Pierce's. The production of horse machines and pulpers ceased, but spares for many Pierce-manufactured machines were still available from old stocks for the following ten years. On 16 July 1965, 124 men were laid off permanently, including staff from the forge, paint shop, wood shop, edge tool, machine shop, foundry, fitting shop and stores.[89]

Clock over entrance to foundry. (Courtesy of management, Tesco, Wexford)

Over the next few years the factory changed hands again and was purchased by Frank Cruess-Callaghan and Owen Conway in 1981, and later in 1984 purchased the spring-making firm of Springs Ltd, amalgamating the two firms to the Pierce complex at Mill Road. In 1997, the firm was trading as Pierce Engineering Ltd, employing 120 workers concentrating on sheet metal fabrication; springs; general engineering; subcontract; waste handling materials; chains and edge tools. The only surviving link with the original Philip Pierce & Co. Ltd was the manufacture of shovels, spades and slash hooks.[90]

On 27 July 2006, *The People* newspaper carried the following report:

Many a tear has been shed over the past few weeks as the crumbling edifice of Pierce's Foundry, once the mainstay of the Wexford economy, was finally reduced to rubble. In its place Tesco Ireland is to build a state-of-the-art supermarket, the new replacing the old, a poignant symbol of the town's industrial heritage making way for the service industry jobs on which Wexford has become dependent in recent years. A former employee of the foundry said, 'It's certainly the end of an era it was part of Wexford's industrial scene for many, many years and no amount of severance pay can compensate for the loss of jobs'. Another person told the press reporter that Pierce's had been part and parcel of Wexford since the 1840s and he would view its demise with a certain degree of nostalgia, a lot of people made a living out there, reared a family out of there and have relatively happy memories about it.

The industry established by a very far-seeing, inventive blacksmith from the village of Kilmore is fading into folk memory, which in its day was the foremost manufacturer and supplier of agricultural farm machinery at home and abroad. Situated on the ground floor of the Tesco Ireland store is the only visible item of memorabilia remaining today. It is the large clock that stood sentinel over the entrance to the foundry, and counted down the daily hours of labour for hundreds of men who passed through its portals during its 125 years of production.

— 9 —

A PIPING DYNASTY
The Rowsome Family

Ireland has given us many famous *uilleann* pipers over the centuries, from John Cash, Patsy Tuohy and Rev. Canon James Goodman to latter-day exponents such as Johnny and Felix Doran and Seamus Ennis. In his book *The Story of the Bagpipe* (1911), Dr W.H. Grattan Flood gives the origins of the *uilleann* pipes as c.1588, while William Shakespeare refers to 'woollen' pipes in his play *The Merchant of Venice* (Act iv, Sc. 1). Shakespeare's reference is most likely a corruption of *uilleann* or elbow pipes. During the 1500s, the playing of the *píob mór* [91] was forbidden by law but eventually resulted in state pardons for those silenced pipers in 1601. Among those pardoned were four Wexford pipers, namely Bryan MacGillechrist, Fergus O'Farrell, Donal O'Farrell and Patrick O'Farrell. [92] It was from c.1715 that the standard of pipe making improved to some degree, with the music of the pipes enjoying great popularity. Many people took up the pipes, and notable among the performers were Lawrence Grogan of Johnstown Castle, [93] who as well as being a fine exponent of the pipes was also a noted composer. From Clone, near Ferns, came Thomas Rudd, a gentleman farmer who was a piper of considerable merit and was an early contemporary and friend of Samuel Rowsome. The name of Rowsome has come down through the annals of traditional Irish music performers for over six generations, producing *uilleann* pipers and pipe makers of the highest calibre. The Rowsome family would be regarded as one of the only families to achieve this remarkable feat of pipe playing since the early decades of the nineteenth century. Originating at Ballintore, Ferns in the barony of Scarawalsh, County Wexford, the Rowsomes farmed in the area and had considerable land holdings.[94]

Samuel Rowsome (1827–1914) was a fine piper and was to be seen at Patron, race meeting and fair where he met and played music with many of the wandering musicians of note at those venues, swapping and learning new tunes which extended his repertoire all the time. He was an acknowledged piper of great ability, who possessed the added talent of being able to repair from bellows to reeds the various sets of pipes which were brought to him for restoration. It was Samuel Rowsome who refurbished Thomas Rudd's pipes following his death, and in turn they were played for many years after by John Cash.[95] Rowsome was highly regarded as a fine jig player and often boasted of his collection of over 100 of such rhythmical tunes. He was a great friend of John Cash, the travelling piper, and Jemmy Byrne, the piper from Shangarry in County Carlow, from whom Rowsome received tuition on the pipes. He sent his sons – John, Thomas and William – to study music under Professor Frederick Jacob Blowitz, a German bandmaster with the Ferns Brass Band.[96] Samuel Rowsome was married to Mary Parslow of Ballyhaddock, who was one of the finest dancers in the area and an excellent violinist. The census of 1911 shows Samuel Rowsome at 84 years of age living with his son, John, and his family at the home place in Ballintore.

John Rowsome (1865–1953) was the eldest son of Samuel Rowsome and farmed the family land at Ballintore. He was a fine musician and learned to read musical notation from Herr Blowitz, as did his brothers William and Thomas. John was proficient on the cornet, on which he played Irish jigs as well as William could play on the violin. Farming absorbed a lot of John's energies, yet he found time to repair and reed many sets of pipes in the south of Ireland. He taught the art and skills of piping to all who cared to learn, as his father did before him. Some nine years after the death of his father, John left County Wexford for Canada in 1923. He became an official of the International Paper Mills in Quebec. John worked up to his eightieth year and took up playing the pipes again up to his death in 1953. He is buried at Côte-des-Neiges, Montreal. A local newspaper report stated on his death, 'he was one of the last of the great Irish uilleann pipers, and the last of the three famous brothers, who were noted performers on this instrument'.

William Rowsome (1868–1928) was a carpenter by trade who moved to Dublin and later married Bridget Murphy from Boolavogue. They set up house at 18 Armstrong Street in Harold's Cross. It was there that William commenced a pipe-making workshop, where he manufactured sets of *uilleann* pipes and carried out repairs to old-time instruments in various stages of dilapidation. William was best known as a fiddler, but also made his mark as a fine performer on the pipes. As well as repairing pipes, Rowsome maintained the organ in Rathmines Church. William played his music in a staccato style and at a very lively pace. During a visit to Ballintore in the summer of 1911, he amazed his family and friends by his use and command of the regulators on the pipes. His staccato was described as a marvel of dexterity and his 'tipping' and 'tripling'[97] were admirable and demonstrated his full use of the pipes. In 1906, the famous collector of Irish music, Captain Francis O'Neill,[98] paid a visit to William Rowsome and recollects how he was favourably impressed by his manner and music. William and Bridget Rowsome had seven children, of whom Samuel, Leo and Thomas were to make their mark in the world of piping. William Rowsome died in 1928 and is buried in Mount Jerome Cemetery, Dublin.

Thomas Rowsome (1870–1928), the third brother of the Rowsomes of Ballintore, was highly regarded as a wonderful exponent of the *uilleann* pipes. He took lessons from his father, Samuel, and was greatly influenced by James Cash, son of John Cash. Cash often visited and stayed at the Rowsome household in Ferns. Thomas was renowned for his renditions of 'slow airs' and in 1899 was awarded first prize at the Dublin Feis Ceoil for his playing. It was said that his playing of single jigs was hard to beat. Thomas moved from Ballintore to Dublin, where he held a prominent position with the Dublin Corporation as sanitary officer. In Dublin he made a name for himself in the world of music, playing engagements at concerts, and in London, Glasgow and other English cities. Standing over 6ft in height and of a genial and kindly nature, Thomas never married.

He died in Hume Street Hospital, Dublin in July 1928, aged 58 years. He is buried with his brother William and other family members at Mount Jerome Cemetery, Dublin.

Samuel Rowsome Jnr (1895–1951) was the older brother of Leo and Tom, and son of William Rowsome of Ballintore and Dublin. Samuel learned to play the pipes at 12 years of age under the tutelage of his father. He was highly regarded and proficient in both chanter and regulators and his performances won him many prizes in competition, even at 16 years of age. The set of pipes played by Samuel were made by his father and were concert pitch and full of tone, which blended very well with fiddle and piano in ensemble playing. Samuel worked as a clerk in Dublin. He was just 56 years of age at his death in 1951.

Leo Rowsome (1903–70) was the best known of the Rowsome dynasty and is often referred to as Rí na bPíobairí,[99] a very fitting title for he had all the attributes of the master musician. He was a wonderful piper, pipe maker and craftsman. Leo Rowsome's sound was instantly recognisable. Clear, vibrant and perfectly pitched tones filled even the largest concert hall. His regulator accompaniment was truly amazing and added to the overall effect of the music by clever and expert use of the harmonic notes available to him. He devoted his life to making, playing and teaching the *uilleann* pipes and taught in the Municipal School of Music for fifty years. Leo possessed a skill learned from his father, that of writing out the tunes for his pupils in a quick and easy manner, thus building up a huge collection of the best tunes for his students' benefit. Among his hundreds of pupils were Willie Clancy, Peter Browne, Paddy Moloney and Liam O'Flynn. Leo also taught at the Piper's Club, Thomas Street,[100] Dublin on Saturday nights. He never drove a car and travelled to all his classes by bus from his home in Belton Park, Donnycarney. His pipe-making workshop was at the rear of his house, where he made full sets of pipes using only the finest materials, ebony, ivory and silver. The only piece of machinery he used was a wood-turning lathe. His wife, formerly Helena Williams (1912–86) of Taghmon, played an essential and pivotal role in supporting her husband in his work to ensure the survival of the *uilleann* pipes. She made hundreds of pipe bag and bellows covers, which adorned and added the finishing touches to a set of pipes. Following his uncle Thomas's success, Leo also won first prize in the Dublin Feis Ceoil in 1921. He played a major role in the formation of Comhaltas Ceoltóirí Éireann and the first Fleadh Cheoil held in Mullingar in 1951.[101] Leo Rowsome was one of the very few professional pipers of his day. He took great pleasure in dressing formally for his concert engagements and his name became known the length and breadth of Ireland as a master piper, pipe maker and pipe teacher. On the centenary of his birth, his daughter, Helena, had 428 of his reels and jigs published by Walton's, Dublin[102] in 2003. It was while adjudicating at the Fiddler of Dooney[103] competition in Sligo in 1970 that Leo Rowsome died suddenly, aged 67 years. He is buried with his wife at Consealy Cemetery, off the Malahide Road, Dublin.

Thomas Rowsome (1906–74) was brother of Samuel Jnr and Leo, and was an accomplished *uilleann* piper, who played and broadcast on national radio with the Rowsome Pipes Quartet in the 1920s. Members of the quartet varied in personnel from time to time, with the original ensemble comprised of Michael Padian, Leo and Tom Rowsome and Eddie Potts. The Potts family originated in Duncormack, County Wexford[104] and also had a strong piping tradition. Tom Rowsome was a founder member of the Thomas Street Piper's Club and Comhaltas Ceoltoirí Éireann. Tom didn't play in public that often, but devoted his time to his business and family. Aged 68 years, he died in 1974.

Leon Rowsome (1936–94) was the son of Leo Rowsome and brother of Liam (violinist), Helena (pipes/tin whistle) and her twin sister Olivia (piano). Leon was born in 1936 and was educated at CBS. Marino, St Joseph's, Fairview and University College Dublin (UCD). He took a B.Comm. Degree and a teaching post as a vocational teacher in Rathdowney, County Laois. Leon started learning to play the pipes at an early age with lessons from his father. At school, Leon often played at school concerts and other functions. He was a member of the Marino School Band, where four of his contemporaries were John Sheehan, composer of the *Marino Waltz*, Paddy Moloney, leader of the Chieftains, Proinsís ÓDuinn, who became conductor of the RTE Orchestra and Leon's brother, Liam, an excellent violinist and adjudicator. Following in his father's footsteps, Leon also taught the pipes on a part-time basis at the College of Music in Dublin. He also made sets of pipes in his father's workshop and became an expert reed maker. As a performer, he was a member of the pipes quartet playing with such piping maestros as Seán Seery, Willie Clancy, Tommy Reck (whose family originated in Oylgate, County Wexford) and Michael Tuohy. In the 1960s, Leon recorded his first album on the Walton label, *Glenside*, and some years later made a second album for Dolphin Discs. An excellent pianist and piano accordionist, he made many broadcasts with the Ballinamere Céilí Band. In the last decade of his life he played very little in public due to ill health. He was married to Nóirín Ní Flaitheartaigh from Ballyfeiriter, County Kerry, and they had one son and four daughters. Leon Rowsome died on 7 April 1994.

Kevin Rowsome (1963–) is a son of Leon Rowsome, and was taught to play the pipes by his grandfather, Leo, when he was 6 years old. Following

William Rowsome (1868–1928) son of Samuel Rowsome, Ballintore, Ferns Co., Wexford. A carpenter by trade, William had a uilleann pipe making workshop in Dublin. Photograph – Irish Minstrels and Musicians, Captain Francis O'Neill, Chicago, 1913.

his grandfather's death in 1970, he was tutored by his own father, Leon. Just like his Ballintore ancestors, Kevin learned to play clarinet and saxophone with the famed Artane Marching Band. This involvement was a huge benefit and broadened his musical horizons. In 1986, Kevin took a two-year career break from his day job and studied woodwind musical instrument making at the London College of Furniture. This experience enabled him to focus on his musicianship and to perfect the family skills of making *uilleann* pipes. Kevin gained public recognition of his playing by winning several awards at Oireachtas na Gaelige. He is widely regarded today as one of Ireland's finest *uilleann* pipers. Like his father, Kevin has vast experience as a performer and instructor of the pipes, with performances in Europe and America. He has served as a staff instructor at the Willie Clancy summer school in Milltown Malbay, the Gaelic Roots Festival in Boston and the Augusta Festival in Elkins, West Virginia. Married to fiddle player Lorraine Hickey, the couple perform regularly as an *uilleann* pipes and fiddle duet.

The Rowsome family dynasty of pipers has covered five generations to date. A sixth generation has commenced, with Kevin Rowsome's two nephews playing the pipes. It is certain that other family members of this new generation will carry on this extremely important tradition of making and playing *uilleann* pipes, thus ensuring the survival and popularity of one of Ireland's traditional musical instruments for posterity. It is gratifying to know that the Rowsome name and tradition is alive and well, and flourishing in the descendants of Samuel Rowsome of Ballintore, Ferns, County Wexford, where it all began over 190 years ago.

10

THE GENTRY IN COUNTY WEXFORD

Lord and Lady Fitzgerald

The Normans landed on Irish shores in 1169, and over the following 400 years the Normans, or their descendants, built stone castles in most of County Wexford. According to William H. Jeffrey in his *Castles of County Wexford*, a collection of notes on castles, he estimated that 235 castles were in existence across the county.[105] Many of those castles have disappeared over the centuries and the descendants of the original occupants built fine stately mansions on the estates. In his illustrated history of *100 Wexford Country Houses*, Dan Walsh gives a brief, yet detailed, account of those fine mansions, their architectural highlights and the people who occupied them.[106] One example is Castleboro, a classical house designed by Daniel Robertson and built for the first Lord Carew, which on completion of the building, cost a massive £84,000 in 1858. During a less peaceful time in Ireland's history many mansions were burned down, with Castleboro suffering this fate, leaving just a ruined shell. Now in its second edition, *Houses of Wexford*, a large tome researched by historian Eithne Scallan, with excellent line drawings of the houses by David Rowe, is a wonderful reference for fine houses, mostly demolished or in ruins, across County Wexford.[107] Many of the houses and their estates were known by the surnames of their owner/occupants, namely: Beatty's of Borodale; De Rinzey and Dundas of Clebemon; Doyne of Wells; Ely of Loftus Hall; Leigh of Rosegarland; Richards of Solsboro; and Tottenham of Tottenham Green. Bargy Castle, supposedly built by Harvey de Montemarisco or some other early Anglo-Norman settler, is still occupied and maintained by the Davison family. One of County Wexford's most notable castles is Johnstown Castle, situated on an estate of c.1,000 acres located 4 miles from the town of Wexford. The last occupants of the castle were Lord and Lady Maurice Fitzgerald, with Lady Maurice in residence up to her death in 1942.

The Right Hon. Lord Maurice Fitzgerald, his Majesty's Lord Lieutenant and Custos Rotulorum of the County of Wexford,[108] was second son of Charles William, 4th Duke of Ireland and Marquis of Kildare and premier Duke of Ireland, and of Caroline Sutherland Leveson-Rower, third daughter of the Duke of Sutherland.[109] He was born at Carton House, Maynooth, on 16 December 1852. On 13 April 1880, he married Lady Adelaide Jane Frances Forbes, eldest daughter of the Earl of Granard, KP, and Jane Colclough Grogan-Morgan at Longford.[110] Having finished his education, Lord Maurice spent eight years in the navy, and went round the world with the Flying Squadron, commanded by Sir Edward Hornby. He returned to his home at the beginning of the Franco-Prussian War, and remained at Carton House for seven years, until his marriage. During this period he was made Captain of the Kildare Militia, which he resigned when he left the county. Lord Maurice, previous to his marriage, was a keen sportsman, and hunted regularly with the Kildare, Ward and Meath hounds in those days. He was accounted the hardest rider in the countryside, and an all-round lover of sports, including shooting. Lord Maurice was well known to be a crack shot. He settled down at his charming residence at Johnstown Castle, and for the duration of his residency to his death, never absented himself from his Wexford home. He pursued the life of an ideal Irish nobleman, in every sense, and resided permanently upon his estate, seldom going out of Ireland except for a few weeks every year, and devoting himself to the service of his country and its people.

Soon after his arrival in Wexford he was offered the Hon. Colonelcy of the Wexford Militia, but he declined the office, as he thought others were more deserving of it. In 1883, His Lordship was appointed High Sheriff, but he resigned after the Spring Assizes, as there was some question of the legality of his holding that position with the Lord Lieutenancy. He acted as foreman of the Grand Jury for one year only, but was on several other occasions requested to do so, and declined, as he wished that Colonel Alcock or Mr Doyne[111] should act in that capacity. Lord Maurice was a singularly liberal and broadminded member of his class. He was entirely free from bigotry or intolerance, and above all things he was fearless and courageous in giving expression to and maintaining his opinion on all questions that might arise, always recognising the right of others to differ from him, and never for a moment attributing base or sinister motives to those with whom he disagreed. For a long time he took an active interest in the proceedings of the Wexford Poor Law Board and District Council, and with Lady Maurice helped to make the lot of the sick and aged poor in the Wexford Workhouse much more comfortable than it had previously been. The comforts of the aged and afflicted in the hospital that the guardians did not see their way to provide, Lord and Lady Maurice provided themselves at their own expense. The Catholics of the county owe Lord Maurice a great debt of gratitude for the fearless manner in which he championed their rights at the County Infirmary Board. More than 90 per cent of the patients in the County Infirmary have always been Catholics, yet not an official of the establishment belonged to the Catholic religion. Catholic patients felt they were deprived of the means to have the last rites administered to them in their dying moments, as the majority of the nursing and administrative staff were of a different religious persuasion. Lord Maurice Fitzgerald at once took up the matter, and with all his might set himself to see that justice was done to the thousands of poor Catholics who sought relief in the County Infirmary. This he succeeded in doing after a prolonged and severe struggle.

When local government was established with the Local Government (Ireland) Act 1868, Lord Maurice was unanimously co-opted a member of the County Council, and every member of the council and every elector in the county was pleased to see him as a member. As a landlord he was considerate and fair, and during the great land agitation the tenants on the Johnstown properties enjoyed peace and comfort while others were treated to hardship and turmoil. It was in Johnstown that Lord Maurice was seen as a most devoted husband and father, and he never tired of doing acts of kindness for his poorer neighbours. The charity shown in a material manner by himself and Lady Maurice was well known, but it was always done in a quiet, unobtrusive manner. Lord Maurice served on many committees in County Wexford, including the Society for Prevention of Cruelty to Animals in the role of president.[112] He was a governor of the lunatic asylum at Enniscorthy[113] and a member of the Her Majesty's Prison Wexford's Visiting Committee[114] and an *ex-officio* guardian of the Board of Guardians, Wexford Union.[115]

On Wednesday, 24 April 1901, the citizens of Wexford were profoundly shocked by the sad news of the death of Lord Maurice Fitzgerald, the popular Lieutenant of the County. Lord Maurice passed away after a very brief illness. The public could scarcely realise the sad and almost sudden occurrence, for His Lordship had been in Wexford on the previous Saturday, and had taken an active part in the proceedings of the Wexford District Council and afterwards, when in the town, appeared to be in his usual excellent health, except that he was a little pale, which was attributed to his recent attack of influenza. On his arrival at Johnstown, late in the evening, he complained of earache, and on Sunday became very ill; on Monday and Tuesday he grew rapidly worse of an affection of the brain. The family physician, Dr Hadden, considered His Lordship's condition so serious that Sir Thornley Stoker, the eminent Dublin surgeon, was wired for and, if necessary, would perform an operation. Sir Thornley Stoker arrived on Wednesday morning, and pronounced his lordship's condition hopeless, adding that he had but a few hours to live. Lord Maurice passed away at 2.30 in the afternoon, having lost consciousness several hours previously. Lord Maurice had been suffering with influenza and Lady Maurice was also suffering with influenza, and had just recovered when her devoted husband was so suddenly stricken down with his fatal illness.

The funeral was strictly private in accordance with his own and Lady Maurice's wishes. This fact was very disappointing to the public, who were most anxious to pay Lord Maurice a last sad tribute of their respect, and would have made such an imposing cortège as had never before been witnessed in south Wexford. The interment took place in the family private cemetery in the demesne. The chief mourners were Lady Maurice Fitzgerald, Gerald Hugh Fitzgerald (son), Geraldine and Kathleen (daughters), Lord Walter Fitzgerald and Lord Henry Fitzgerald (brothers), Lady Eva, Lady Mabel and Lady Nesta Fitzgerald (sisters), Col Fitzgerald,

Lord and Lady Maurice Fitzgerald. (Courtesy of IAMA, Johnstown Castle)

CB (brother-in-law), Mr and Mrs Colles (cousins), Mr William B. Nunn and Mr Crozier, family solicitor. The coffin was of plain polished oak, lined with satin, and contained the following inscription: 'Lord Maurice Fitzgerald, Born 16/12/1852, Died 24/4/1901.'[116] He was just 48 years of age.

Captain Gerald Hugh Fitzgerald, 4th Royal Irish Dragoon Guards, only son of the late Lord Maurice Fitzgerald and Lady Maurice Fitzgerald, Johnstown Castle, Wexford, married Dorothy Charrington, youngest daughter of Spencer Charrington, Esq., Winchfield Lodge, Hants at Tidworth Church, Hants, England on 5 August 1914 as reported in the *Enniscorthy Guardian*, 8 August 1914. The marriage had been previously arranged to take place in September of that year, but owing to the war crisis, which necessitated the departure of Captain Fitzgerald with his regiment abroad, the former arrangements were abandoned, and the function was of a quiet nature. Earlier that year, Gerald's sister, Kathleen Fitzgerald, married Major Michael Lakin, MHF, Carrickbyrne House, youngest son of Sir Michael Lakin, Bt, and Lady Lakin of Warwickshire on

Saturday, 18 July 1914 at 1.30 p.m. at St Brigid's Church, Rathaspeck. The Lakins set up home at Carrickbyrne for a time, following their marriage, and later took up their new residence at Horetown House near Foulksmills, County Wexford.[117] Joy turned to sadness on 13 September when a telegram from the War Office, London to Johnstown Castle announced the death of Captain Gerald Hugh Fitzgerald, killed in action at Aisne-Oise near the village of Bourg-et-Comm, France.

Johnstown Castle, Co. Wexford. (Gaul Collection)

The Lakins had two sons from their marriage: Gerald Michael, born 17 January 1916, and Maurice Victor, born 30 October 1919, much to the delight of both parents and in particular to their grandmother, Lady Maurice Fitzgerald. In 1930, the great joy and happiness experienced by the Lakin family of Horetown House was to turn to sorrow and bereavement, following a tragic hunting accident and untimely death by which a husband lost his wife, and two young boys lost their mother. Thirty-eight-year-old Kathleen Lakin rode out with the Wexford hounds on Friday, 21 February, and while hunting near the village of Gusserane her mare stumbled in the act of clearing a 4ft ditch and dislodged Mrs Lakin, sending her crashing onto her back on the hard surface of the roadway. She struck her head and never moved after that. She was in a serious condition and was removed at once to the County Hospital. Sir William de Courcy Wheeler, the distinguished surgeon, travelled from Dublin and everything possible was done for the unfortunate Mrs Lakin, but to no avail. She died without ever regaining consciousness about 3 o'clock on Sunday afternoon. Once again, a gloom had been cast over the home of Lady Maurice Fitzgerald of Johnstown Castle by the tragedy that befell her daughter, Kathleen, and the Lakin family.

Lady Maurice Fitzgerald survived her husband by forty-one years, during which she kept the huge Johnstown Castle Estate operational with the managerial skills of her first cousin, Captain Ronald Forbes. Through the tragedy of the loss of her only son and one of her daughters, and witnessing the Great War and the onset of the Second World War, Lady Maurice Fitzgerald immersed herself in a myriad of church, charitable and social activities with an energy that belied her advancing years. She was the daughter of the 7th Earl of Granard and sister of Lady Sophia Grattan Bellew, widow of Sir Henry Grattan Bellew of Castle Forbes, Longford and a half-sister of the Earl of Granard. Lady Maurice was a niece of the Hon. Mrs Deane-Morgan of Ardcandrisk. For many years she took a very active part in public life in the county and carried on the good work and traditions her late husband had established. She was chairman of the Board of Guardians, of the Wexford Branch of the National Society for the Prevention of Cruelty to Children, and of the County Wexford Horticultural Society. She took a prominent part in the Women's National Health Association. There was virtually no organisation across the county for the relief of the often terrible conditions affecting the general public, and especially the poor, to which she did not give her support and allegiance. During the Great War she acted as chairman of the Wexford Branch of the Queen Mary Guild, and in 1914 she opened the Wexford Cinema Palace at a concert and moving picture show in aid of the Belgian refugees. Always ready and willing to offer her generous support to every appeal or to make a donation in a quiet and private manner, she gave a great deal of employment at her estate and kept a large staff at Johnstown. Her active interest in the Rathaspeck Nursing Association provided a district nurse in the Rathaspeck area. As a trustee of the Lady Esmonde and Cullimore charities, she succeeded in obtaining from the High Court an order which helped the Sisters of St John of God in nursing the poor of the town of Wexford. She always expressed an interest in the town and its progress. Lady Maurice's half-brother, the Earl of Granard, was Deputy Speaker of the House of Lords in 1915 and was also a member of the first Irish Senate. He had served as Postmaster General in England from 1906 to 1910.

In her final year, Lady Maurice Fitzgerald was confined to bed for months prior to her death, aged 82 years, which occurred at her residence, Johnstown Castle, on 18 November 1942. Her funeral took place in the family private burial ground within the grounds of the Johnstown Castle Estate, in the presence of her daughter Mrs More-O'Farrell, her cousin Captain Ronald Forbes, her son-in-law Major Michael Lakin, and other family members. Funeral arrangements were carried out by Messrs John Sinnott and Sons, Funeral Undertakers, South Main Street, Wexford.[118] The great estate of Johnstown Castle was without her lord and lady with the demise of the wonderful and caring Lady Maurice.

The Act of 1945 was an agreement made on 28 December 1944 between Dorothy Violet Jefferies of Carrigbyrne, Adamstown (The Settler) and Maurice Victor Lakin of Horetown, Foulksmills, County Wexford, and the Minister for Agriculture whereas the lands, tenements, hereditaments and premises hereto formerly part of the Family Estates.

The document for the transfer of all properties and land at Johnstown Castle be presented to The Nation as a Free Gift for the purposes hereinafter mentioned. The preliminary arrangements in relation thereto should be specified in writing in the form of an Agreement between Dorothy Violet Jefferies and Maurice Victor Lakin and The Minister. The document was signed and witnessed by Dorothy Violet Jefferies and Maurice Victor Lakin in the presence of their legal advisors. A list of the properties on The Estate was shown and a list of employees that were retained and those whose services were no longer required and wages and compensatory amounts are listed together with additional privileges enjoyed by those employees while working on The Estate. All documents for the First and Second Schedule were signed by Dorothy Violet Jefferies, Maurice Victor Lakin and D. Twomey. (*Johnstown Castle: A History*, Liam Gaul, The History Press, 2014.)

It was the end of an era.

11

POLITICIANS AND A SOLDIER
The Redmond Brothers

The Redmond family are one of the oldest Anglo-Norman families to settle in County Wexford and held considerable acreage of land until they were dispossessed in the mid-seventeenth century. They turned their interests to commerce and shipping.[119] In 1770, John Redmond was a famous banker who lived at Somerton, Wexford, and established a private bank, known as Redmond's Bank, in the Bullring. Married to Elizabeth Sutton, daughter of John Sutton, Summerhill, Wexford, they had two sons: Patrick Walter (1803–69) of The Deeps and John Edward (1806–65) of Newtown, Co. Wexford, a Justice of the Peace and a Member of Parliament for Wexford, from 1859–65. Married to Margaret Archer, daughter of Dr Nicholas Archer, they had no family. He is buried in St John's Churchyard, John Street, Wexford.[120] Patrick Walter Redmond was the father of William Archer Redmond (1825–80), MP for Ballytrent, Co. Wexford and grandfather of John Edward Redmond MP (1856–1918), and William Hoey Kearney ('Willie') Redmond MP (1861–1917) was brother of John Edward Redmond MP.[121] Both brothers served as Irish Parliamentary Party MPs until their deaths.

JOHN EDWARD REDMOND (1856–1918)

John Edward Redmond was born on 1 September 1856 at Upper Rutland Street, Dublin, and was the eldest son of William Archer Redmond and Mary

Hoey of Dunganstown, County Wicklow.[122] In 1858, the Redmond family moved to Ballytrent House,[123] near Carnsore, Co. Wexford, where John Edward was raised and spent his childhood to 1868, when he left for Clongowes Wood College, where he had a most successful academic career excelling in debating and drama. His portrayals of Macbeth and Hamlet were lauded as the finest performances ever given by the greatest actor ever seen at Clongowes Wood. One of John's teachers, Fr Keane, described him as a very mature character.[124]

In 1873, Redmond entered Trinity College, Dublin, to study law and only stayed for one year, not having made great progress with his studies. He was 19 years of age in 1875, and from then until 1880 very little is known of him, except he became involved in the political outlook of Charles Stewart Parnell having attended his first political meeting with him. He also spent a lot of time in the House of Commons, apprenticed to his father, William Archer Redmond, MP for Wexford Borough, at the same time studying law, eventually working there as a parliamentary clerk. On his father's death in 1880, John Edward Redmond had his mind set on succeeding him for the Wexford Borough seat. It was not to be, for Parnell requested Redmond to stand aside in favour of Tim Healy, who took the seat. However, Redmond's turn came, when at 24 years of age he was elected to the Borough of New Ross in February 1881. Noisy and rowdy scenes heralded his entry into the House of Commons. He was duly sworn in and within twenty-four hours made his maiden speech, and with twenty-six other Home Rulers was suspended from the House of Commons.[125]

John Redmond had immersed himself in a group of young supporters of Parnell, and in 1882 he was asked by Parnell to set out on a fund-raising mission to Australia and New Zealand. With his brother, Willie, he travelled across those vast countries collecting monies for the Home Rule cause. The tour raised a massive £15,000 for the party and the National League. While in Australia, John and Willie met with the Dalton sisters in Sydney. The sisters were from a well-to-do family of Irish immigrants to Australia. John married Johanna Dalton. The brothers returned via the United States of America, travelling through the country organising and addressing large audiences as part of their campaign. The amounts of money generated in America were small, as Parnell had fallen out of favour with the Fenian movement there.[126]

Left: John E. Redmond. (Courtesy of Co. Wexford Public Library Service)

Right: Major Willie Redmond. (*Trench Pictures from France*)

In the general election of 1885, John Redmond was elected as Member of Parliament for North Wexford. He was 29 years of age. He served as party whip when the first Home Rule Bill was introduced to the English Parliament in 1886 by William Gladstone. The Bill failed, so Redmond became actively involved in the Plan of Campaign, which was a land war seeking rent reductions for farmers in difficulties trying to pay their rents. In 1888, Redmond was jailed for five weeks in Tullamore Jail resulting from activities by the Plan of Campaign movement. Sad news was announced in 1889: the sudden death of Johanna Redmond, having given birth to a stillborn child in Dublin. John Redmond was left with two girls and a boy – Esther, William and Johanna – all under the age of 6 years.

The Home Rule Party split following the divorce case which high-lighted Parnell's affair with Katherine O'Shea in November 1890. Gladstone announced that he could not lead the Liberal Party in a Home Rule alliance while Parnell remained leader. Tim Healy was totally opposed to Parnell's leadership, motivating Redmond to hold a pro-Parnell rally in Dublin. The split in the party and John Redmond's support for Parnell meant Redmond lost many of his old political colleagues, and his political career in Wexford was finished. Parnell contested three by-elections, unsuccessfully, aided by Redmond from October 1890 to his final attempt at Carlow in July 1891. In October, just three months follow-ing his final defeat, Charles Stewart Parnell was dead. This left John Edward Redmond as the only one of Parnell's supporters suitable to lead the dwindling Home Rule Party. Soon after Parnell's death, Redmond reluctantly resigned his Wexford seat and contested a by-election for Parnell's vacant seat in Cork City – which he lost. In Waterford City a few months later he stood against Michael Davitt, and won the seat which he would hold for the next twenty-seven years, up to his death.[127]

The call for the passing and adoption of the Home Rule Bill would have meant Ireland having its own domestic parliament rather than govern-ance from Westminster. The two Home Rule Bills put before the House of Commons in 1886 and 1893 were defeated. Following the 1910 elec-tions, the Irish Parliamentary Party was led by John Edward Redmond and they held the balance of power in the House of Commons. This position enabled the Irish Parliamentary Party to bargain for a third Home Rule Bill to be introduced in exchange for supporting the Liberal Party, who were in government. The Liberal Party passed the 1911 Parliament Act, which reduced the House of Lords' delaying power of veto to two years. On 11 April 1912, the Third Home Rule Bill was introduced and passed by the House of Commons by a small majority. However, the House of Lords rejected the Bill by an overwhelming vote, which happened again in 1913. Edward Carson and the Irish Unionist Party fiercely opposed the Home Rule Bill and in 1912 in excess of 500,000 signatures were registered by the Ulster Covenant against passing the Home Rule Bill. The following year, the Ulster Volunteer Force was formed to oppose the Bill, by military force if necessary. The Third Home Rule Bill would have made provision for a two-chamber Irish parliament with a 164-member House of Commons and a 40-member Senate, all allowing Ireland the continuation of MPs being elected to Westminster. The provisions of the Home Rule Bill became law on 18 September 1914, but simultaneously another Act was passed preventing the Bill becoming law until after the First World War.

On the outbreak of war, John Redmond pledged the Irish Volunteers to the defence of Ireland. On his return home to Ireland on the Sunday morning, Redmond set out for his home at Aughavanagh, Co. Wicklow. He stopped his car at Woodenbridge, in the Vale of Avoca, where he encountered an assembly of the East Wicklow Volunteers. Present were the two Wicklow MPs and Colonel Maurice Moore, Inspector General of the Volunteers. John Redmond, in a short impromptu address to the group, outlined their duty:

> to go on drilling and to account yourselves as men, not only in Ireland itself, but whenever the firing-line extends, in defence of freedom and of religion in this war where it would be a disgrace forever to Ireland, and a reproach to her manhood if young Irishmen were to stay at home to defend the island's shores from an unlikely invasion.

Redmond's Woodenbridge speech became better known than his manifesto on this subject. Redmond pledged the Irish Volunteers to the defence of Ireland and called on Irish men to enlist in the army.[128]

John Redmond was now 60 years of age in 1916, two years after the onset of the war, when the Easter Rising erupted in Dublin. This was a shattering blow to Redmond's lifelong policy of constitutional action. In the following year further sad news arrived in Wexford: his younger brother, Major Willie Redmond MP, had been killed in action in Flanders on 7 June at 56 years of age. Years of disappointment, frustration with governments, personal and general family tragedy dogged John Edward Redmond's life up to the time of his relatively early death, aged 62, on 6 March 1918 in London.[129]

Two of the local Wexford newspapers printed the following tributes to John Edward Redmond. This was the headline of *The Free Press* in its edition of Tuesday, 12 March:

Death Of The Irish Leader Mr. J.E. Redmond passes away, The nation plunged into grief.

The death occurred in a London Private Nursing Home at 7.45 a.m. on Wednesday 6 March of John Edward Redmond, MP and Chairman of the Irish Parliamentary Party.

Remains to be Interred in Wexford.

Mr. Redmond's remains were conveyed to Westminster Cathedral on Wednesday night where Requiem Office and High Mass, at which Cardinal Bourne presided, was held on the following day. The remains were brought by sea to Kingstown (Dunleary) arriving on Friday night and John Edward Redmond's final journey was by special train to Wexford on Saturday morning for burial. His remains were accorded a public funeral in his native town. Following Solemn Requiem Office and High Mass in the Church of the Immaculate Conception, Rowe Street at 11 o'clock the dead Leader was laid to rest in the Redmond vault in John Street Churchyard. The cortege passed through the principal streets of the town. In the order of the procession – The Clergy preceded the bier, which was surrounded by a guard of honour of the Irish National Foresters in costume, immediately followed by the relatives. Members of Parliament and Public Organisations, Corporation and Councils and the Redmond Memorial Committee followed next. On Saturday morning all business was suspended in town until after the interment, demonstrating that the citizens by closing business establishments and drawing blinds paid a last tribute to the dead leader.

From *The People* newspaper:

Death of John Edward Redmond MP

Deep mourning marked the death of John Redmond

When the Irish leader, John Edward Redmond, MP died unexpectedly in a London nursing home last week, Ireland was plunged into mourning especially amongst his fellow loyal followers in his native Wexford. He had succumbed to heart failure after an operation.

The editorial in the local *The People* newspaper stated:

Now, more than ever will the people of Ireland realise the loss that they have sustained in the death of this great Irishman. The sole ambition in his life was to win national autonomy for his country. He laboured strenuously to this end; indeed, no one can realise the terrible strain it must have been on Mr. Redmond for so long to direct the movement for attaining Home Rule. The terrible burden he had to bear, particularly of late, had so told upon his robust health that recently death was pictured in his face. And this was brought about by the treachery of those in high places whom he trusted and of a certain section of his countrymen at home who stooped to the foulest epithets to level against one who was a patriot above everything else. We refer to the small cliques of small minds who levelled the most odious charges of treachery against him, one who devoted his entire life to working so strenuously for the betterment of his country and his countrymen. That he was a thoroughly honest man and always acted for the best, will be conceded by the overwhelming majority of Irishmen. As we have pointed out, the course of events for some months past has shown that even if he had pursued another line of policy, as his critics have pointed out, it is now clear that Ireland would not have been granted Home Rule in face of the opposition of Ulster.

MAJOR WILLIAM HOEY KEARNEY (WILLIE) REDMOND (1861–1917)

William Hoey Kearney Redmond was born on 15 April 1861 and grew up at Ballytrent, County Wexford. William was the second son of William Archer Redmond and Mary Hoey, daughter of General R.H. Hoey of the Wicklow Rifles and the 61st Rifles. The Redmonds came from a Catholic gentry stock of Norman descent, and were associated with County Wexford for over seven centuries. William's father was a Home Rule Party MP for Wexford Borough for eight years to 1880.

Willie Redmond, as he was known, was five years junior to his brother John Edward Redmond, leader of the Irish Parliamentary Party. Like his father, Willie Redmond was educated at Clongowes Wood College from 1873–6, having previously attended at Knockbeg College and St Patrick's College, Carlow. On finishing his education he was apprenticed on a merchant sailing ship, later taking a commission in the Wexford Militia, the Royal Irish Regiment, in December 1879. He had thoughts of a regular army career but resigned in 1881. He joined the Irish National Land League and was arrested in 1882 for possession of seditious literature, which led to imprisonment for three months in Kilmainham Gaol, with Charles Stewart Parnell, William O'Brien and others. Redmond was a loyal supporter of Parnell. With his brother, John, the Redmonds made a journey to Australia in a fundraising campaign for the Land League. The brothers met and later married two Australian sisters by the name of Dalton. Willie married Eleanor Mary Dalton in February 1886 and they had one son, who died in 1891, aged 5. His wife lived until 1947. Willie Redmond was called to the Bar in 1891 but never practised, living for most of his life on a salary from the Irish Parliamentary Party. Willie Redmond was elected, in his absence, as MP in his father's Wexford Borough constituency and took his seat in the House of Commons of Great Britain and Ireland. The Wexford Borough constituency was abolished in 1885 and Redmond was then elected MP for Fermanagh North, and in 1890 was elected MP for the Clare East constituency and held the seat until his death. He had served as an MP for the Irish Parliamentary Party for thirty-four years.

The Great War began on 28 July 1914 and lasted for four years to 11 November 1918, and was one of the deadliest conflicts in history, involving an estimated 70 million military personnel and resulting in millions killed and wounded. Many Irishmen were called to enlist in the Irish regiments by the leader of the Irish Parliamentary Party, John E. Redmond MP, as he believed that the participation of Irishmen in the 10th and 16th Irish Divisions of the British Army would strengthen the cause for the implementation of the Home Rule Act. The possibility of this Act being passed had been suspended for the duration of the war. The call to arms was answered by many Wexfordmen, including John Redmond's brother, Willie Redmond, who at 53 years of age was one of the first Nationalist Volunteers to enlist. Willie Redmond played a huge part in the recruitment campaign, speaking at numerous venues throughout Ireland. At a venue in Cork city he referred to himself as: 'grey haired and old as I am, come with me to the war for if Germany wins we are all endangered'. Redmond felt it might serve the cause if he was also in the firing line, and was one of five Irish MPs serving with the Irish Brigade. At the outbreak of the Great War, Willie Redmond was commissioned as a captain in the Royal Irish Regiment, his former regiment of thirty-three years previously. He went to France in the winter of 1915–16 with the 16th Irish Division and was engaged in action, earning a mention in dispatches from Sir Douglas Haig. He received the rank of major on 15 July 1916, a promotion which took him away from the action. While on leave from his war duties he made a speech in Parliament in March 1917, demanding that England introduce the suspended Home Rule Act considering Ireland's involvement and the sacrifice of Irishmen's lives in the war. Early in June 1917, Willie Redmond returned to the front.

Major Willie Redmond, now 56 years old, obtained special permission to join his battalion, 'A' Company of the 6th Battalion, Royal Irish Regiment. Preparations were in readiness in Belgium for the Battle of Messines, and on the night before the planned assault of 7 June 1917, Redmond visited every company of the 6th Battalion and is said to have 'spoken to every man'. The following day the Irish troops of the 16th and 36th divisions advanced in the attack on the Messines Ridge towards the village of Wijtschate. Major Willie Redmond was one of the first out of the trenches and, on going over the 'top', he was hit in the wrist and then in the leg. Although wounded, he urged his men on. A short distance away from the fallen major, Private John Meeke of the 36th Ulster Division's 11th Battalion Royal Inniskilling Fusiliers was searching the battlefield for wounded soldiers. Meeke, had seen the major fall and made his way over to him and tended his wounds. Both men came under heavy fire, resulting in Private Meeke receiving a wound to his left side. Seeing the young soldier bleeding quite badly, Redmond ordered him to return to the British lines, which the Ulsterman refused to obey. Meeke was hit a second time but still refused Major Redmond's order to return to the British lines. Repeatedly fired on, the two men were eventually rescued by a patrol from the 36th Ulster Division. Major Redmond was taken from the field of battle to a Casualty Clearing Station located at a hospice in the grounds of Loker Catholic Convent. Suffering from shock and his wounds, Major Willie Redmond died that afternoon despite the efforts of field surgeons.

The nuns buried his remains in the grounds of the hospice, and three months later a special service at the graveside was attended by Irish leaders and members of the 16th Irish and 36th Ulster Divisions. Further battles raged over the area, and the hospice was destroyed but later rebuilt on a new site near the village of Loker. Willie Redmond's grave was moved to the nearby war cemetery. At the request of the Redmond family, the grave was once again moved to a spot outside the cemetery, where it is still tended today. There is a plaque in the Dublin Four Courts with the following inscription: 'In memory of Irish Barristers who fell in The Great War 1914–1918'. Included in the list of names is that of William Redmond. His name is also inscribed on the House of Commons panel as Major W.H.K. Redmond, killed.

Private John Meeke from County Antrim was awarded the Military Medal for his remarkable act of bravery in tending the wounded Major William Redmond under heavy enemy fire. Meeke died in 1923 and was buried in an unmarked grave and forgotten until 2004, when a memorial stone was erected, by public subscription, at Derrykeighan Old Graveyard, County Antrim.[130]

The Redmond family's involvement in politics did not end with the death of John Edward Redmond, as his son, William Archer Redmond (1886–1932) was elected as Irish Parliamentary Party MP for East Tyrone serving from 1910–18 and for Waterford City from 1918–22. He was elected as an Independent TD for Waterford from 1923 until his death in 1932. William Redmond's wife, Bridget (Mallick) then held the seat for Waterford from 1933 until 1952. The Redmonds were elected MPs to the House of Commons from banker and magistrate John E. Redmond as a Liberal MP for Wexford from 1859 to John Edward Redmond's son, William Archer Redmond to 1922, a total of sixty-three years.

~ 12 ~

MASTER MUSICIAN
Dr William Henry Grattan Flood

D r William Henry Grattan Flood lived thirty-three of his 71-year lifespan in Enniscorthy where he served, to his death in 1928, as organist at St Aidan's Cathedral. Grattan Flood was born in Lismore, Co. Waterford on 1 November 1857, one of four brothers and an elder sister, Agnes. Prior to going to college, William received his earliest education from his maternal grandfather, Andrew Fitzsimons, who operated an academy for boys preparing for entrance to Mount Mellery College. He received musical education from his early years from his mother's sister, Elizabeth Fitzsimons, and was considered something of a prodigy. A very good pianist, he was invited by the Duke of Devonshire to give a piano recital at Lismore Castle. The young William was only 9 years of age at that time. He also received private tuition in music from Sir Robert Stewart (1825–94), Professor of Music at the University of Dublin.[131]

Grattan Flood was educated at Mount Mellery College, All Hallows, the Catholic University and Carlow College where he spent some years studying for the priesthood. He left the seminary and went on to become Professor of Music in the Jesuit Colleges of Tullabeg and Clongowes Wood and later at St Wilfrid's, Cotton Hall, Staffordshire. On his return to Ireland he taught at St Kieran's College, Kilkenny, and St McCartan's College, Monahan.[132] He was so proficient at the organ that he became organist of St Peter's Pro-Cathedral, Belfast, at the age of 19. He later became organist at Monaghan Cathedral, Thurles Cathedral and for a time he was conductor of the D'oyly Carte Opera Company. He was also bandmaster of the 104th Regiment, being the last civilian army bandmaster in Ireland.[133] Finally, he was appointed organist at Enniscorthy Cathedral, Co. Wexford, in 1895, where he settled down. He played the organ at St Aidan's Cathedral for thirty-three years, to be succeeded by his daughter, Kathleen, who held the post for twenty-nine years until her death in 1957. Father and daughter had given a total of sixty-three years in the service of the church.

W.H. Grattan Flood was a noted writer, composer and historian, and among his published contributions are: *The History of Enniscorthy* (1898), with a new edition in 1916; *The Story of the Harp* (1905); *The Story of the Bagpipe* (1911); *The History of the Diocese of Ferns* (1916); and *A History of Irish Music* (1927). Among his musical compositions were: *The Mass of St Aedan in Bb*; *The Mass of St Carthage in A*; *The Mass of St Wilfrid in G*; and *A Benediction Service* dedicated to Pope Leo XIII. In his book *A History of Irish Music*, Dr Grattan Flood covers all aspects of our native music, from ancient Irish music to the musical instruments used; Irish music in the Middle Ages; O'Carolan and his contemporaries; Irish pipers in the eighteenth century; and he even has a chapter devoted to George Frederick Handel and Dr Thomas Arne and their musical sojourns in Ireland. He dedicated this very comprehensive tome to Edward Martyn, the founder of the Palestrina Choir, Dublin.[134] As well as *The Story of the Harp*,[135] he also published a very scholarly and extensive twenty-five-chapter work on the bagpipe from the earliest biblical references in the Book of Genesis and Nebuchadnezzar's band referred to in the Third Book of Daniel. Greek and Roman bagpipes, ancient Welsh pipes, early English pipes and the Scottish Highland pipes are all dealt with, and of course the ancient and native Irish warpipes and *uilleann* pipes.[136] This book has been a source of reference for many collectors and writers on the music of the pipes up to the present day.

A devout Catholic, Grattan Flood contributed many articles to various ecclesiastical reviews, journals and periodicals and composed the music for 'The Hymn to Christ the King', or as we know it by the opening words, 'Hail! Redeemer, King Divine!' The text was by Father Patrick Brennan C.SS.R.[137] His *Mass of St Aedan in Bb* was in honour of St Aidan or Maodhóg, the first Bishop of Ferns. It was Grattan Flood who originally

The Enniscorthy Christmas Carol, staff notation. (Computer generated by Liam Gaul)

compiled the names of all the bishops of Ferns as transcribed in their Latin forms on the pillars of the central tower of St Aidan's Cathedral.[138] His other two Masses are dedicated to St Carthage, Patron of Lismore, and St Wilfrid, Patron of St Wilfrid's in Staffordshire, England, respectively. In his lifetime, Dr W.H. Grattan Flood was honoured with papal honours by four popes. His degree of Doctor of Music, *honoris causa*, came on 1 November 1907 from the old Royal University, later to become the National University of Ireland.

In recent times there have been many recordings and arrangements made and published of the Enniscorthy Christmas Carol. It was collected by William Henry Grattan Flood in the Enniscorthy area c.1911. The carol is deemed to have mediaeval origins and is simple in construction. The words of the carol give the full Christmas story in its verses. The melody has a distinctive Irish flavour. It was Father Patrick Cummins (1881–1942),[139] administrator at St Aidan's Cathedral, Enniscorthy, who drew Grattan Flood's attention to the old carol. Father Cummins, a native of Coolamain, Oylgate, brought Grattan Flood to hear his mother sing the carol. Grattan Flood noted the lyric and transcribed the melody into musical notation. The carol was taught to the children of St Aidan's National School, Enniscorthy, the first children to sing the carol. It was very quickly taken up by many singers in the area and its popularity spread, with priests going abroad from the House of Missions in Enniscorthy. A transcript of the carol by Grattan Flood was sent to Oxford University, who were in the process of gathering lesser-known and popular carols for publication in 1928. It appears as Carol No. 14 and is titled as 'Wexford Carol' in the *Oxford Book of Carols*, together with various footnotes.[140] At the same time, Grattan Flood submitted another carol to the *Oxford Book of Carols*, simply titled 'Irish Carol', which is given as Carol No. 6. The air for this carol is a variant of the Irish song 'Tá an coileach ag fógairt an lae'.[141] Credit for the survival of the Enniscorthy Christmas Carol must be attributed to Dr Grattan Flood for collecting and sending it to Oxford for inclusion in their prestigious book of carols.

Grattan Flood was a prolific writer and contributor to a multitude of musical, historical and church journals, with numerous publications to his credit. He edited a new standard edition of *Moore's Irish Melodies*, *The Spirit of a Nation* (1911), edited the music of *The Armagh Hymnal* in 1915 and selected *Airs of O'Carolan* (1917). In 1922 he wrote a booklet, *Introductory Sketch of Irish Musical History*, and *Early Tudor Composers* was published in Oxford in 1925. He also published *Memoirs of Vincent Wallace*, the Waterford-born composer of 'Maritana', and Michael William Balfe, composer of the opera 'The Bohemian Girl', and the inventor of the nocturne – John Field. He also composed the songs 'Irishmen All' and 'Our Loved Ones Far Away' to words by T.D. Sullivan. He composed many madrigals, part songs, hymns, piano solos, marches and transcriptions for church organ.

William Henry Grattan Flood lived at his residence, Rosemount, Enniscorthy, where his death occurred following a few days illness on 6 August 1928. He was in his seventy-first year. His remains were buried in the New Cemetery, Enniscorthy, and are surmounted by a limestone Celtic cross with a Celtic harp and the following inscription: 'Erected to the memory of Chevalier William Henry Grattan Flood, Enniscorthy in recognition of his invaluable services to Irish Music and Literature, August 6th 1928'. A second inscription, an epitaph, is by his friend Sir Alfred Perceval Graves (1846–1931), who wrote these lines: 'Two Irish orators of rival fame, Combine to mould his memorable name; But music was his first love and his last; And links in him our present with our past.'

— 13 —

THE IRISH COUNTRYWOMEN'S ASSOCIATION

Anita Lett

It was in 1908, when two women met on a train journey from Dublin to Enniscorthy, County Wexford, that a conversation between Mrs Anita Lett and Mrs Alex Rudd led to the foundation of a women's national organisation originally known as 'United Irishwomen'. Two years later, on 8 May 1910, a meeting was convened by a small group of well-educated women in Bree, County Wexford, in the residence of Anita Lett, at which this germ of an idea became a reality with the foundation of United Irishwomen. Non-denominational and non-party political, this organisation proposed to offer support, friendship and hope to all women in rural Ireland, many of whom experienced lives of constant hardship and drudgery. These rural difficulties could only be alleviated by education, which became a key-word. Classes and demonstrations of vegetable growing, poultry and egg production, cheese making, fruit bottling and beekeeping were arranged, all of which could add to the self-efficiency of rural households. All of this knowledge also brought a marked improvement in people's health, with a much better and more varied diet from nutritious food. The sale of surplus produce generated an added income for the household budget and gave a new independence to rural women.[142]

At that first meeting, Anita Lett introduced an outline document entitled 'The Scheme Explained', which gave an insight into the aims and objects of the United Irishwomen. This scheme advocated a coming together and unification of Irish women, regardless of social class or religious belief, for the 'common good of the country'. Anita believed that such an organisation could vastly improve the quality of Irish rural life for women and their families, and bring an end to emigration and bring prosperity to Ireland with a happy and contented population.[143]

Anita Lett formed a committee under the presidency of Lady Power of Edermine, on which farmers and labourers' wives, along with the 'county families', were represented. A set of rules were drawn up and the United Irishwomen began in the small village of Bree, County Wexford,[144] with its first official meeting at St Aidan's Hall on 15 June 1910.[145] It was expected that Anita Lett would have been the organisation's first president, but the honour fell to Lady Power. Lady Power was a member of the famous and influential whiskey distillery family and they had been responsible for a lot of local development, including funding for the building of Edermine Bridge across the River Slaney some years earlier. Anita Lett was elected vice-president with a Miss Quinn as secretary and treasurer. A further nine ladies from the surrounding areas formed the elected committee. Many friends from neighbouring country houses, including Alcocks of Wilton Castle, Carews of Castleboro, Roches of Enniscorthy Castle, Furlongs of Scoby House, Bryans of Borrmount, Fitzgeralds of Johnstown Castle and Powers of Edermine House were all extremely supportive of this new organisation. Other farming families were foremost in joining Anita, including Hasseys, Staffords, Warrens, O'Neills, Wickhams, Creanes, Roches, Johnsons, Regans, Mullets, and many more.[146]

A flower show was held at Bree on 20 August 1910, generating the necessary funds to run the organisation, and they were soon able to make a contribution to the running costs at St Aidan's Hall.[147] The Jubilee nurses at that time provided a nursing service only in towns, with no such nursing care and attention being available to women in rural areas. The United Irishwomen in Bree recognised this need and sent two women, Margaret Cowman from Sparrowsland and Annie Foley from Dranagh, to train as nurses in London. On completion of their training they would return to work as district nurses in the homes around Bree.[148]

The organisation blossomed and spread very quickly through the dedication and hard work of Anita Lett and her group of helpers and organisers.

Branches or guilds were established throughout County Wexford, and gradually expanded nationwide. In early December 1910, a second branch of United Irishwomen was formed at Davidstown, and by the following year there were seven branches in Ireland. They had a motto which stated: 'Relief from all our troubles will only come from within ourselves. Don't wait to be helped – do it yourself.'[149] As with all organisations, the United Irishwomen had its own constitution to govern it and outlined its aims and objects:

- The Society consists of a central union and branches; the whole governed by an Executive Committee.

- The work of the central union is first of all to organise the women of Ireland by the formation of branches, as the parent body of the co-operative movement has been largely succeeded in organising the men.

- Those wishing to join the central union as individual members are proposed and seconded by existing members and are elected by a majority of votes at a meeting of the Executive Committee.

- Their annual subscription is *2s 6d*.

- Branches are formed in rural districts comprising all the women of the neighbourhood and are governed by a committee composed of a president, vice-president, honorary treasurer, honorary secretary and twelve members.

- Each branch pays an affiliation fee to the central union of 5s and each member of a branch pays a subscription of 6*d* to her branch.

- The Executive Committee is composed of representatives of the branches and individual members who meet in Dublin and deal with all questions that concern the Society.

Anita Lett was elected as first national president, a position she held for just two years, to be replaced by those who realised the benefits of her organisation but felt better qualified to run the organisation themselves.

Left: Anita Lett, founder of the ICA, portrait.

Right: St Aidan's Hall, Bree, Co. Wexford.

Anita now devoted all her energies and efforts to the Bree Guild, focusing on the betterment of rural women in County Wexford. Her many charitable schemes and organisational abilities were always foremost for the United Irishwomen. One of her ideas was promoted on 11 December 1911 at an executive committee meeting, where she suggested a need for funeral cars in poor areas. The scheme was rejected on a first hearing, but was later put into practice. In an effort to promote all things Irish, in 1913 Camogie games were organised by Anita for members of the United Irishwomen. She personally supported and trained the very successful Davidstown-Bree Camogie team, which won the District Final beating Tombrack.[150]

In 1928, together with Mabel Rudd from Ballycarney, she established a co-operative named Slaney Weavers. Local women were supplied with spin-ning wheels and worked in their own homes to produce top quality tweed, another source of added income for the members. The tweed that was pro-duced was collected at the Enniscorthy Co-operative Society on a weekly basis. With the assistance of her sister, who lived in Newbury, Berkshire, England, Anita set up a sales outlet for the finished tweed cloth.[151]

Anita Georgina Edith Lett, née Studdy (1872–1940), was born at Waddeton Court, a large manor house, near Brixham in South Devon. She was the daughter of Henry Studdy, a former clergyman and commander in the Royal Navy. He died in 1880. Her mother, Amelia Margaret Crapper, remarried W. T. Summers of Esthlen, Newmarket. Anita was small in stature, slender with straight hair usually worn in a bun.[152] Anita came to Borodale House, County Wexford, as a nurse to Captain David Longfield Beatty. As time passed a romance ensued between Anita and the captain, resulting in their marriage in 1899. They had one son, Henry Longfield Beatty.[153] Anita was 28 years of age when she married Captain Beatty. He was 30 years senior to her.[154] Her marriage to David Beatty was never acceptable to the Beatty family, and when she was widowed in April 1904 she was forced to leave Borodale. A plot of land was given to her on the farthest part of the estate. She made a house on the estate habitable and bought c.46 acres from the Kehoe family, her near neighbours. In 1908 she remarried Harold Lett, a member of a well-established farming family. Harold Lett's ancestor had arrived in Ireland as a captain in Oliver Cromwell's army in 1649, and his family settled in Ballindara, Bree and Kilgibbon, County Wexford. Harold and Anita Lett had two daughters from the marriage, Eithne and Anita, known as Peggy.

The connection of Anita with two very prominent families, the Beattys and the Letts, together with her own personality, opened many doors for her in the many projects she started. Her own gifts at arts and crafts, and in particular gardening, ensured that her many ideas and concern for the welfare of the community were generally accepted. She and her husband lived the life of landed gentry, where hunting was a major activity in the area. Anita enjoyed 'following the hounds' as she was an expert horsewoman and on horses generally. The Letts fox hunted with the Bree Harriers. At the time she founded the United Irishwomen, both her husband and herself were interested in rural politics and co-operatives, and Anita was vice president of the Wexford Farmers' Association. With her brother-in-law, Charles Lett, she kept up her interest in beekeeping. Charles Lett was very involved for years in the Enniscorthy Beekeeping Association.

Oylegate ICA 1910–2010, sculpture by S & N Granite Ltd, Camolin. (Photograph by Aidan Quirke)

Anita Lett's last local appearance was at a Christmas party in the Bandroom, Davidstown, which was organised by the United Irishwomen for the local children. During the party, Anita distributed Christmas gifts to the children from the candlelit Christmas tree. Anita's husband Harold died on 25 January 1938, and following a few days' illness Anita died on 5 June 1940. For both of their burials they had requested simple traditional funerals, where their respective coffins were placed on straw-covered farm carts and drawn to the burial place by horses devoid of pomp or ceremony. Harold and Anita Lett are buried in St John's Church of Ireland graveyard in Clonmore, Bree.[155]

The United Irishwomen changed the name of the organisation to the Irish Countrywomen's Association (ICA) in April 1935. An organisation that began in the small village of Bree in County Wexford in 1910 has spread to every one of the twenty-six counties of Ireland, with 500 guilds and approximately 10,000 members. Their national headquarters is located at Merrion Road, Dublin, and their adult education centre is at An Grianán, Termonfeckin, Co. Louth. Translated as 'the Sunny Place', An Grianán is the first residential adult education centre in Ireland. The manor house was built in the eighteenth century by the McClintock family and at that time was known as Newtown House. An Grianán was officially opened in October 1954 by the President of Ireland, Seán T. O'Kelly, and Dr Donal O'Sullivan, Director of the Folk Music Department at UCD. Courses available cover cookery, arts, crafts, leisure and personal development with live-in accommodation, if required. Anita Beatty Lett, a pioneer in the founding of the United Irishwomen organisation, has left a legacy which is still vibrant today as the ICA.

14

IRISH CHAMPION PUGILIST
Jem Roche

James (Jem) Roche was born in Ballinclay, Glynn, on 5 September 1878. His parents were John and Mary (Moran) Roche. His brother, Laurence, was born on 17 June 1880 at Scoughmolin, Murrintown. Eventually, the Roche family moved to Wexford town, where his sister and two other brothers were born. Jem attended the Christian Brothers School where, apart from his academic studies, he displayed a big interest in sport and music. Jem played trombone with the Holy Family Confraternity Brass and Reed Band in Wexford town.[156] The family had strong patriotic tendencies, and Jem's grandfather had fought in the Battle of Three Bullet Gate during the Insurrection of 1798.[157] The young Roche became a member of the Young Ireland's Gaelic Football Club which were based in Selskar, an area of Wexford town, where he was one of the club's star players.

Having finished at school, Jem was apprenticed to the blacksmith's trade at William Haughton's forge in Abbey Street in Wexford town. On completing his apprenticeship, Roche left the forge in Abbey Street and for a number of years was a journeyman smith, travelling to wherever the work was available. He most likely worked as a blacksmith at Mike Carton's forge at Scarawalsh, and later in Cleariestown at Willie Carroll's forge.[158] Jem Roche's blacksmith's skill was well known and his great strength was manifest when wielding the heavy sledgehammer.

During a boxing tournament at the Town Hall in Cornmarket in Wexford town, one of the principal fighters listed on the tournament card failed to show up, so the 18-year-old Roche was prevailed upon to step into the boxing ring to make up the fixture. Although the young boxer was inexperienced in the sport, he faced a well-known local pugilist with great determination and spirit, and the young blacksmith succeeded in winning the fight by a knockout. Jem Roche was now launched on a boxing career that brought him fame and success in the ring, both in Ireland and abroad.

A rather small man, at 5f 7in, Roche weighed in at just under 13 stone yet he fought all of his bouts as a heavyweight boxer. These statistics were an advantage in a way, as they allowed Roche to use his great strength and speed to dodge his many opponents' punches, retaliating with solid counterpunches and often bringing a bout to an early close by a clear knockout. In those early years of his career, Jem Roche fought mainly in local County Wexford tournaments and at contests in surrounding counties. He soon became a favourite with the large number of supporters of this very popular sport. At 24 years of age, in 1902, Roche became heavyweight champion of his native County Wexford by his defeat of Pat Connolly in a fifteen-round bout. Connolly was the reigning champion at that time.

World Heavyweight Championship, Jem Roche and Tommy Burns.

In London, later that same year, Roche knocked out Tom Davis in the third round of a heavyweight contest. Returning to Dublin, he fought two further bouts. His first opponent was Jem Clarke,[159] followed later by a middleweight bout with Jack Fitzpatrick.[160] A number of other top-class fighters, including the US amateur heavyweight champion, Joe Hagan, hit the canvas in a whirlwind series of contests. In 1904, Roche was defeated by another heavyweight champion of the British Army and Navy, Private Harris, by a knockout in the twelfth round. By 1905, Jem Roche was ranked as one of the foremost heavyweight boxers in the world and defeated the British Army champion, Corporal McFadden, by an knockout in the twelfth round on 24 April 1905 in Dublin, and the American boxer Charlie St Clair on 7 August by a knockout. Later, in September and December of that same year, Roche had two bouts with 'Young' John Sullivan in Dublin, losing the first contest to Sullivan and winning the second contest by a technical knockout. Roche did lose some bouts over his fighting years. He was managed by Nicholas J. Tennant,[161] who recorded Roche's record as 30-7-1 with twenty-three KOs.[162]

Jem Roche was very well known and popular across Wexford town and county. Possessed of a modest and good-humoured nature, he paid regular visits to chat with his blacksmith friends at local forges. Other days he visited the town's Main Street, where he would mingle with shoppers, or the quays, where he conversed with fishermen or sailors arriving home into port. He enjoyed the publicity he received in the various sporting sections of newspapers both in Ireland, the UK and America. One American columnist described Roche as a born boxer, while another American newspaper stated, 'The Irish Champion is very popular in Ireland and Great Britain where his fame is spreading like an epidemic'.

In 1908, the sole topic of conversation in Wexford town was the 'Big Fight' due to take place in Dublin on St Patrick's Day. Roche was the favourite to win the World Championship, and a lot of money was wagered on the Irish contender. A train full of supporters departed from Wexford to be present and to witness a great victory for Jem Roche. Letters and messages had been pouring in to Roche from all over Ireland wishing him well. Even his opponent, Tommy Burns, sent a message: 'Give Roche my regards. Tell him I hope the best man wins.' Commenting, Roche replied: 'Burns is a master of the art and is in great condition.'[163]

It was evident that this contest with the World Champion, French Canadian-born Tommy Burns,[164] would prove Roche's worth as a heavy-weight boxer. An American syndicate headed by Richard 'Boss' Croker[165] was going to back the Irishman and arranged the match. This much-awaited bout was scheduled for St Patrick's Day, 17 March 1908, at Dublin's Theatre Royal. Tommy Burns was a larger-than-life character enjoying great popularity, and was a born showman. Prior to taking up boxing, Burns had been a professional hockey and lacrosse player. Like Jem Roche, Burns was a small man of 5ft 8in and weighed in at 12½ stone, but was a perfectionist in all his enterprises and was extremely knowledgeable in his chosen sport. He had even written a book on the art of boxing, *Scientific Boxing and Self Defence.*

Mr John Mellifont Walsh, proprietor of *The People* newspaper, commissioned William Redmond as its Special Representative to travel over to London where Burns had his training quarters in Jack Straw's Castle, Hampstead, in a successful bid to secure an interview with him. The following is a resume of Redmond's report for *The People* newspaper.

One of Jem Roche's 'seconds' stated that Roche had never trained as hard for any fight as he did for that one. The same can be said of Burns, who looked on the Irishman as a formidable opponent. Tommy Burns had learned from Charlie Wilson, a fighter who had suffered a heavy defeat by Jem Roche, of his forthcoming opponent's strength and punching power. At that time Burns was viewed as a wizard of the ring, and it was suggested that he indulged in the occult sciences and practised hypnotic or mesmeric influences on his opponents in the ring. Be that as it may, had Jem Roche succeeded in getting over the first round, there's no telling how that fight would have gone. Burns was determined to get rid of him as quickly as he could, and had evidently known of the weakness in Jem's anatomy, which was over his left eye. In the course of his Homeric battles, Roche had sustained a severe cut over it, and when Burns opened up the fight, he held his fists high up and had them moving in weaving fashion as if he were indulging in mesmeric passes, whilst he continued an encircling movement and treaded his way in and out. Then, availing himself of an opening caused by Jem lunging with his left, he flashed in a short-arm right twisting punch, which caught Jem between the left ear and eye, and he sank to the ground. It could not be described as a fall; he was on his elbows and knees, but his head rested on the floor of the ring. As if to shake off the stunning effect of the blow, he rocked and struggled to raise himself by the aid of the ring ropes, but slipped back again, and by the time he got to his feet, ten had been counted. No one was more surprised than Burns at the swiftness of his victory; his deftly delivered punch for which he was famous – and it never travelled so far – had rendered the Irishman incapable of rising in time to continue the fight. This chance blow had deprived him of his prospects in the World's Championship Contest.[166]

The result was a great disappointment to the audience. Consternation and disbelief reigned, to think that the Irish Heavyweight Champion had crumpled with such ease. One man ran out of the theatre onto the street declaring to all and sundry, 'Roche is murdering him', as he tried to sell his ticket to a passer-by. Public opinion was sympathetic to Jem Roche, believing that he was a far better boxer than Burns and had he not fallen foul of a lucky punch, he would have proven his worth as the fight pro-gressed. Later, Roche's response was simple and honest: 'I was just feeling my way before he caught me – testing his methods and sizing him up – when he sent over a twisting right which upset me.'[167] It was the shortest World Heavyweight title fight in history, lasting just eighty-eight seconds. Jem Roche continued to fight through 1909 to 1913, but never got a return fight with the World Champion.

His courage as a fighter was never more fittingly demonstrated than when he met 'Cyclone' Billy Warren, a huge black boxer. Compared with Jem, he was a mountain of a man in physique, and he was possessed of a right-hand punch which was devastating – he connected that with Roche's jaw in the third round of a fight in Belfast on 9 July 1909. So great was the strength behind it that it lifted the Wexfordman completely off his feet, and as he fell, his head struck the boards and he was rendered unconscious. On a return bout in Dublin on 26 August, Roche fought Warren for twenty rounds, giving his opponent such a belting that he almost knocked his mouth com-pletely out of shape.[168]

TO PERPETUATE THE MEMORY OF
JEM ROCHE, WEXFORD,
UNDEFEATED IRISH BOXING CHAMPION
WHO DIED 28. Nov. 1934.

"A GREAT FIGHTER, GREAT SPORTSMAN,
BUT GREATER STILL
IN HIS OWN SIMPLICITY & MODESTY."

ERECTED BY HIS MANY ADMIRERS.
HUGHES

Commemorative plaque, Bullring, Wexford.

On his retirement from professional boxing, Jem Roche had a public house opposite the present Dún Mhuire Theatre on South Main Street, Wexford. His motto was: 'Only Champion Drinks Served.'[169] In his spare time he helped train local boxers and footballers, and was also involved with the training of the County Wexford football team that won the 1918 All-Ireland Championship. He sold the public house after some years and became a bookmaker, and was a familiar figure on racecourses and greyhound coursing fields.[170]

He also retained his blacksmith's forge in Slaney Street, Wexford, and at one stage founded a boxing club in Selskar which proved to be a saviour for many Wexford youngsters, keeping them from taking the 'wrong road' in life. Jem Roche was not only Wexford's boxing hero throughout his life, but he also won a provincial football medal with the Young Ireland's football team. All through his life he enjoyed great popularity and was well loved by the people of his town for his cheerful and good-natured temperament. He was appointed manager of a commission agent, a job he worked at until his death. In the latter months of 1934, he suffered a minor accident in which he cut his foot. He never sought medical attention and walked to work every day, experiencing considerable pain and difficulty.[171] He was eventually taken to Wexford Hospital, where his leg had become gangrenous and it was discovered that nothing could be done to save his life. He died at his home in Ram Street (Skeffington Street) on Wednesday morning, 28 November 1934.[172]

In Wexford there was widespread shock at the news of Jem's death. Huge crowds attended his removal and at his funeral on the Friday morning at the Church of the Immaculate Conception, Rowe Street, where the Funeral Mass was celebrated by Fr Michael J. O'Neill, parish administrator. The funeral cortege was headed by a piper's band and a guard of honour included his former manager, Nicholas Tennant. A lorry filled with floral wreaths was also in the funeral procession as it wended its way through the silent streets to Jem Roche's final resting place at St Ibar's Cemetery. Wexford's mayor and corporation, the Worker's Union of Ireland, Wexford Ex-Servicemen, the County Board of the Gaelic Athletic Association and many other sporting

Jem Roche, Irish Heavyweight Champion in fighting pose (Courtesy of the Roche family)

organisations all paid tribute to Wexford's boxing hero at their specially convened meetings. Jem Roche was survived by his wife Bridget, his daughter, Molly, and four sons: Laurence, John, Pierce and Seamus.

In 1961, a memorial plaque was erected in the Bullring, Wexford, to honour this proud sporting son of Wexford. The inscription reads as follows: 'To perpetuate the memory of Jem Roche, Wexford, Undefeated Irish Boxing Champion who died 28 November 1934. "A great fighter, great sportsman, but greater still in his own simplicity and modesty". Erected by his many admirers.'

Author's Note: The Roche family were extremely talented vocal and musical performers, with Jem's daughter, Molly (Mrs James Turner), a wonderful pianist and accordionist who travelled with her renowned dance band far and wide throughout County Wexford, bringing first-class dance music to many social occasions. Molly's own family also possess fine musical and vocal talents, especially her son, Pierce Turner, musician, composer and recording artist equally popular in the United States of America and Ireland. Jem's son, Pierce Roche, was a fine singer who self-accompanied his songs with the dulcet tones of his piano accordion, and his musical tradition is carried on today by his son, Billy Roche, musician, composer and internationally acclaimed playwright. Mary (Roche) McDonald is a renowned soprano and is the daughter of Laurence Roche. John and Seamus also made their talented contributions to the musical life of their native place. In conversation with Billy Roche, he informed the author that the playing of the trombone passed down through family generations from his grandfather, Jem Roche, to his son Seamus and to his son-in-law, Jim Turner and Jim's son, Seamus, and Billy Roche's brother, Jim, played both trumpet and trombone and all were members of the HFC Brass and Reed Band.

— 15 —

ARTIST, DESIGNER AND AUTHOR

Eileen Gray

Eileen Gray (Kathleen Eileen Moray Smith), daughter of James McLaren Smith and Eveleen Pounden, was born on 9 August 1878, the youngest of five children, into a wealthy Protestant Anglo-Irish family and resided in a Georgian manor at Brownswood, Enniscorthy, Co. Wexford. Her father was a Scottish landscape painter and her mother, Eveleen Pounden, was a grand-daughter of Francis Stuart, 10th Earl of Moray. Following the death of her uncle, Eveleen claimed the title, becoming the 19th Baroness Gray in 1895. Eileen Gray's father left the family residence when she was 11 following her parent's marriage break-up. He moved to Italy to continue with his paint-ing. Baroness Gray changed her children's names to Gray, as did her father, calling himself Smith-Gray. Eileen was educated for a short time in Dresden, Germany, but was educated mainly by governesses. Eileen possessed artistic tal-ents which she was encouraged by her father to pursue. With her father, Eileen travelled throughout Europe, where both father and daughter painted scenes from their expeditions. Her father and Eileen's brother both died in 1900, the same year that Eileen and her mother visited the World Fair in Paris. The most prominent and popular style at that time was art nouveau. In 1901, the 23-year-old Eileen left for London, where she attended the Slade School of Fine Arts, a painting school for high-society youngsters. Her teachers at Slade included Philip Wilson Steer, Henry Tonks and Frederick Brown.[173] The fol-lowing year she went to Paris with Kathleen Bruce and Jessie Gavin to study drawing and enrolled at the Atelier Colarossi, and later the Académie Jullian.

On hearing of her mother's illness, Eileen returned to London to look after her. There she discovered Chinese lacquer work at Dean Charles's restoration workshop, where she was immediately taken on as an apprentice.

In 1907, Eileen returned to Paris and was apprenticed to Seizo Sugawara, a Japanese lacquer craftsman, and adapted traditional Asian lacquer techniques to contemporary Western furnishings. Sugawara was from Jahoji, a village in northern Japan famous for its lacquer work, and was in Paris to restore the lacquer pieces Japan had sent to the Exposition Universale. Eileen Gray was so intent on learning this trade that she was a victim of lacquer disease, which is a very painful rash forming on the hands.[174] It did not stop her from working. In 1910, Gray opened a lacquer workshop with Seizo Sugawara, and by 1912 she was producing commission pieces for some of the richest clients in Paris.[175]

Eileen Gray moved into an eighteenth-century apartment, which she rented and purchased years later, at 21 rue Bonaparte in Paris, which she was to keep until the end of her life. In the 1920s, Eileen was approached by Louise Dany, a country girl, seeking a job as her housekeeper. She became her maid, turned assistant and companion, and remained with Eileen until her death over fifty years later.[176] With a childhood friend, Evelyn Wyld, she travelled to Morocco in 1909 with the aim of learning how to make rugs in the da Silva Bruhns style. Shortly afterwards, she set up her Parisian workshop in rue Visconti. Eileen's lacquer work continued and she exhibited her work at the Salon des Artistes Décorateurs (SAD) in 1913, and a year later the famous couturier Jacques Doucet bought her four-panelled screen *Le destin*, which led him to place further orders for items of furniture from Eileen. Forever looking for 'new' design ideas, she made a journey to Mexico, where she visited Teotihuacan and later used some of the features in one of her Mediterranean houses.

In conjunction with Evelyn Wyld, a life-long friend and business partner who produced Eileen Gray's carpet designs at their studio in rue Visconti, they also designed wall hangings and carpets which they sold at Eileen's newly opened boutique Jean Désert, at 217, rue du Faubourg-Sant-Honoré in Paris, opposite the Salle Pleyel.[177] It was while exhibiting her work at the Autumn Salon that she met Robert Mallet-Stevens, who ordered a rug and some furniture for the Villa des Noailles he was building at Hyères. She was invited to the 14th exhibition of the Society of Decorators, where she presented *Bedroom for Monte Carlo* in 1923. The same year, Léonce Rosenberg submitted to the Galerie de l'Effort Moderne an exhibition devoted to Dutch architecture. This may have been when Eileen met the young architect of Romanian origin, Jean Badovici.[178]

Pierre Chareau invited Eileen Gray to exhibit her work at his stand at the SAD. The Dutch periodical *Wendingen* (turning-points),[179] which was close to the de Stijl movement, devoted an article to Eileen Gray, with an introduction by Jan Wils and an article by Jean Badovici. In 1926, *House for an Engineer* formed just a part of her projected work.

At Cap Martin, Roquebrune, she bought a plot of land in Badovici's name and started to work using models and plans. She studied topography, the sun's trajectory and the direction of the winds. E-1027, which was built for Gray and her lover, Jean Badovici, grew from furniture into a building. She created a number of pieces of loose and built-in furniture for the house and installed others that she had previously designed, always with close attention to their interaction with the senses and the human body. She created a tea trolley with a cork surface, to reduce the rattling of cups, another trolley for taking a gramophone outside, and the E-1027 table, whose height can be adjusted to suit different situations. The house contained the Transat, a kind of exalted deckchair, and the Bibendum, which engulfs you in thick squishy tubes.[180] She built a series of cupboards and storage units with minute consideration of such things as the way that the light falls on their contents, the integration of electrical fittings and radiators, the way that drawers might open on a corner, the arrangement of mirrors that would allow you to see the back of your head. Such thinking expanded into the building, with small windows located to allow a view when lying down, shutters allowing complex modulations of shadow and breeze, and the positioning of a fireplace next to large glass doors so that you can see firelight and natural light at once. A water tank, a humble functional thing, is placed so that it forms a shelter for an external dining area underneath. A rooftop glass enclosure for a spiral stair is a delicate work of steel and glass, also furniture-like. The living room of E-1027 with furniture and rugs designed by Eileen Gray – and, on the far wall, Le Corbusier's mural.

The building is mostly white outside, its interior modulated with planes of slight pink or eau de Nil, or a nocturnal blue or black. These colours are maritime, but subtly so, such as you might see in deep water, inside a seashell or after sunset. There is an acute awareness of surfaces, both inside and out, and their degrees of shine or roughness. On the back wall of the main living space, playfulness being part of her armoury, she placed a large nautical chart. This, she said, 'evokes distant voyages and gives rise to reverie'.

The basic form of the house is a simple cuboid, raised on pillars, but within that she created a series of layers that filter the progression from land side to sea side and from shadows to light. And although its boundaries seem quite definite at first sight, they are dissolved in places by networks of routes and steps that run through the landscape into the house and out again. The building is solid, but can be considered a series of screens placed over the landscape. The house, meanwhile, a fragile-looking thing, endured several forms of violence. Le Corbusier visited and, apparently outraged that a woman could have made such a significant work in a style he considered his own, assaulted it with a series of garish and ugly wall paintings, which he chose to execute completely naked. He would later build a retreat for himself nearby, and was found drowned by the rocks in the Mediterranean below villa E-1027 on 27 August 1965. Between 1926 and 1929, when she built the villa with her partner the architect Jean Badovici, the name of this holiday home they designed together was derived from the interlinking of their initials: E for Eileen, 10 for the J of Jean, 2 for the B of Badovici, 7 for the G of Gray, the name of the villa thus interweaves their initials. Gray and Baldovici had parted in the early 1930s, but the couple were reconciled after the Second World War. Baldovici died of liver disease in 1954, with Eileen Gray in attendance by his death bed. In 1948, Baldovici had tried to reclaim authorship for Eileen Gray's vision from Le Corbusier, and a massive row ensued over the wall murals and they never spoke again. Baldovici had intended putting the house back into Eileen Gray's name in recognition of the fact that she had purchased the site, designed and implemented the construction and gifted him the entire enterprise.[181]

The completed Villa E-1027, Roquebrune-Cap-Martin, incorporated almost 300 separate architectural, fixtures and fittings designs, and the villa is undoubtedly the highlight of Eileen Gray's life's work. Her second piece of domestic architecture, Tempe a Paille, Castellar, which she designed as a retreat for herself, was modern, minimalist and really experimental on all levels.

Very little is known of Gray's emotional life. Characteristically, she burnt all letters and personal mementoes in old age. But it seems that from her early years in France, Gray was on the fringes of the raffish intellectual Paris-Lesbos scene. She had a long, close friendship with Gaby Bloch, companion-manager of the American Marie Louise Fuller, alias Loïe, of twirling dance celebrity.

Eileen Gray in later years, portrait.

She was later to be seen in the company of Damia, the green-eyed, gravel-voiced singer whose popular '*chansons dramatiques et tristes*' had made her the Edith Piaf of her day. Gray escorted Damia to restaurants and nightclubs, elegant in her Poiret evening coats and Lanvin hats. She knew Nathalie Barney, Romaine Brooks and Gertrude Stein. But she never quite joined up with the Café Flore society of Americans in Paris. They were probably too raucous.

Eileen Gray believed in process – an artist who never ceased practising her craft. Almost every major piece of furniture she designed was for somebody she loved. Her art was neither narcissistic nor motivated by self-expression. She designed over 100 other unrealised architectural projects in addition to the three pieces of domestic architecture for which she is best known in the South of France. Gray was a perfectionist and an inventor, and always ahead of her time. Her most commercially successful undertaking was the production of her carpet designs with Evelyn Wyld from 1910 to 1924. Eileen Gray was very loyal to her close friends, and had the gift of being able to forgive her detractors with grace and humility and had a very lively sense of humour. During her leisure time she liked nothing better than to swim and to sunbathe. Of an adventurous spirit, she flew across the Channel with Cheron in his biplane in 1913, and she was one of the first to receive a driving license in Paris. On her 98th birthday, the suggestion was made to her that she might live long enough to receive a telegram from the Queen. Her instant response was, 'But I'm an Irish nationalist!'[182]

In 2009, a small brown leather armchair by Irish designer Eileen Gray, and once owned by Yves Saint Laurent, went for auction at Christie's in Paris for an expected price of £3 million, but despite the global recession the world's richest furniture collectors pushed the price to more than six times the estimate when it realised £19.4 million. This unique piece, known as the 'Dragons Armchair' because of the ornate sculptures on its sweeping armrests, was created between 1917 and 1919. It was the most expensive piece of twentieth-century design ever to be auctioned.[183]

Brownswood Estate near Enniscorthy, Co. Wexford, has a very historical past which spans over 700 years. It is situated in an idyllic setting overlooking the River Slaney, and the actual castle, which pre-dated at least two later houses on the site, was held by the Brown family from the thirteenth to the seventeenth century and gave this area its name. On 27 February 1573, an armed force arrived at Brownswood intent on assaulting McDonagh More McTege. The incumbent of Brownswood, a loyal subject of Queen Elizabeth I, was struck in the head and died instantly. In 1650, the castle was attacked and destroyed by Oliver Cromwell's troops, the remains of which still stand to the present day. In the early nineteenth century the estate came into the hands of Colonel Rochford of Cloughrennan, Co. Carlow. He sold it on some years later for the sum of £5,500 to Captain Jeremiah Lonsdale Pounden. Pounden married Lady Jane Stewart, daughter of the 10th Earl of Moray. The first house on this site appears to have been an elegant Georgian building, although it is not named on the 1840 Ordnance Survey maps, suggesting that the unidentified demesne may at that time have been a relatively modest holding. While Eileen Gray is thought to have been annoyed at the demolition of the old Georgian-style house, all accounts of her childhood stress the cold and discomfort of her family home and her fears and nightmares growing up there. She had left for London and the Slade School of Art by the time her mother took the drastic step of knocking down the old house, and building the mansion which the baroness felt to be in keeping with her new status.

DESIGNS BY EILEEN GRAY

E.1027 Villa

The Bibendum
Armchair

The Transat
Chair

The Dragon
Chair

The Non-Conformist
Chair

Side Tables

Original Brownswood House. (Courtesy of Aidan Ryan, Brownswood)

The very large and elaborately designed house was completed in 1894 to the design of Thomas Drew. Baroness Gray died in 1918, at which time it became the property of her daughter Eileen Gray, who allegedly hated it. Eileen Gray lived mostly in France right up to her death in 1976, and was honoured by Ireland in 1975 by being made an Honorary Fellow of the Royal Institute of the Architects of Ireland.[184]

Eileen Gray died on Halloween 1976. She is buried in the Père Lachaise Cemetery in Paris. Her family omitted to pay the licence fee for burial, so her grave is not identifiable. Eileen Gray, the woman from Brownswood, was a painter, sculptor, photographer, artist, designer and architect – a renaissance artist and the mother of Modernism.

— 16 —

RICHARD CORISH
AND THE CORISH FAMILY

The Corish family from Wexford town has been one of the leading families in County Wexford, involved in local and national politics since Richard Corish was first elected to Wexford Borough Council in 1913, a seat he retained for the rest of his life. That involvement was later continued by two sons, his cousin, his grand-daughter and grand-son.

The name Corish is an ancient name and is derived from the name Bermingham. The Gaelic patronymic MacOrish or Corish was adopted by the Berminghams, who became more Irish than the Irish themselves. The Gaelic equivalent of Piers is Feoras (Corish).[185] This Irish name was also used by the Leinster Berminghams, whose Castle Carbury in Co. Kildare was also called Castle MacFheorais. It was in south Wexford that the Corishes became most numerous in later years. The name Corish has a long and prominent association with the ecclesiastical, farming, commercial and political life of south Wexford.[186]

Peter Corish from Oyster Lane on South Main Street, Wexford, married Mary Murphy from the William Street[187] area in November 1885, and following their marriage Peter and Mary Corish set up their family home at 35 William Street.

Richard Corish was born on 17 September 1886 at his parents' home and was the firstborn of three children. He had two sisters, Mary (1888) and Johanna (1890). Peter Corish, whose family originally came from New Ross, was a carpenter by trade. His own father was a corn buyer also named

Richard, a Christian name carried down in the family by Peter and Mary's firstborn. Richard's mother, Mary, died on 11 January 1893. She had been ailing for some time and was in failing health, and her death was a huge blow to her husband and the three young children. Mary's sister, Johanna Murphy, had been caring for her for some time and eventually took on the role of rearing the children.[188]

The young Corish attended infant school at the Presentation Convent in Francis Street, Wexford, before moving on to the Christian Brothers School at George Street. Richard was an avid reader with a strong interest in history. His sister Johanna was a fluent Irish speaker and later taught at Curracloe School. Richard had an interest in the GAA (Gaelic Athletic Association) and supported his local team – the Mulgannon Harriers – when he lived in that area of the town. As was customary at that time, Corish left school at 14 years of age to seek work. However, he did not follow his father's trade but took an apprenticeship as a machine fitter. He completed his apprenticeship at the Wexford Engineering Works, known locally as the Star Ironworks, where he was employed in the fitting shop.[189]

Richard was influenced in his political philosophy by Michael Davitt, James Connolly, James Larkin and Michael Collins.[190] Corish was a committed socialist.

Richard Corish believed that employers during the 1911 lockout were despots similar to the tyrannical landlords and the stranglehold they had on the tenants and peasantry in the past. It was the local working-class people that Corish was interested in, and the terrible and strict work practices that were inflicted by the employers. Most lived in very poor housing conditions with little opportunity to voice their opinions in local politics. Businessmen and ratepayers controlled local politics. Agitation seemed to be the means for obtaining better conditions and concessions. Industrial strikes were reported not just in Ireland, but also further afield on the Continent.[191]

The lockout occurred between August 1911 and February 1912. Richard Corish did not become involved with the lockout but as an organiser with the ITGWU (Irish Transport and General Workers' Union). The first union representative sent to Wexford during the lockout was P.T. Daly. Jim Larkin also arrived in Wexford on behalf of the union. Then, in February, ITGWU official James Connolly arrived. He ensured a consensus was reached between the employers and locked-out workers, and was instrumental in negotiating the final settlement, thus ending the lockout. Richard Corish was the workers' representative for the Star Ironworks. He was actively involved on the fundraising committee to provide relief for the locked-out workers and their families, helping to organise concerts, GAA matches and other events. During the lockout, Richard Corish emerged as a political leader among the workers and began appearing on the platform at public meetings with Daly, Larkin and Connolly. During his visits to Wexford, James Connolly stayed at Corish's house at 35 William Street.[192]

The ITGWU recruited members very quickly, which brought about the lockout of 700 workers engaged by the owners of the Star Ironworks, Doyle's Foundry and Pierce's. The Wexford lockout lasted all of six months, with the locked-out workers having to survive on 10*s* a week, a very small amount of money on which to feed, clothe and pay rent for their family homes. There were many turbulent public meetings during that time, resulting in hundreds of Royal Irish Constabulary (RIC) being drafted into the town to maintain order and to protect 'blacklegs' brought in to replace striking regular staff. These workers came in from Scotland and England and were housed in a former public house premises, Brien and Keating on Main Street. The premises had been purchased for this purpose by Philip Pierce and Co. On Wednesday, 6 September, a large contingent of RIC reinforcements arrived by train and marched along Wexford quay in a show of strength, where they were confronted by a large angry crowd at Gibson's Lane. A baton charge by the RIC resulted in many injured, with a further baton charge at South Main Street where Michael O'Leary, a 58-year-old corn porter, was a victim of the charge. Mr O'Leary died some days later of septic meningitis. His funeral was the largest seen in the town for many years.[193]

The locked-out workers and the ironfounders eventually reached a settlement, and all the men went back to work in February 1912, having left the ITGWU and joined the newly formed Irish Foundry Worker's Union (IFWU). This 'new' trade union was really a flag of convenience, as the employers would not recognise the ITGWU By 1914, the IFWU was affiliated and completely absorbed into the original Irish Transport and General Workers Union. Richard Corish, as its secretary, had realised his ambition with workers being properly paid for their toil under the protection of a trade union.[194] The lockout was not caused by the foundry workers demanding higher wages. It was about the workers seeking the right to join the union of their choice – the ITGWU. Of course, negotiations for a proper wage and working conditions were top of the agenda after the lockout.[195]

Richard Corish never again resumed his own trade as a machinery fitter, going on to concentrate his efforts on trade union business.[196] He did serve on the executive of the ITGWU and on the Wexford Trades Council and he worked as an insurance agent to supplement his income.[197] He was a co-founder and honorary secretary of St Patrick's Workingmen's Club and contested the local elections, topping the poll as the Labour representative on the borough council in January 1913 and elected an alderman to Wexford Corporation. Richard Corish was elected to the exalted office of Mayor of Wexford in 1920, and held that office without a break for the next twenty-five successive years. In 1921, he gained a seat in Dáil Éireann on a Sinn Féin ticket and was returned to government as a Labour deputy in the 1922 general election, and held the record of never losing an election. As a Sinn Féin TD he was present for the Treaty Debates. He voted in favour of the Treaty. He represented Wexford as a Labour TD from 1922 to 1945, and was a front-bench spokesman participating in many debates on local government, in particular on housing. He served on many committees, including the Greater Dublin Commission and the Poor Law Commission. He was a director of the Irish Tourist Association, president of the Council of Municipal Councils and was representative on the General Council of County Councils, as well as being a member of the governing body of University College Dublin and High Chief Ranger of the Irish National Foresters.[198]

While serving his twenty-fifth year as Mayor of Wexford, in January 1945 he was conferred with the Freedom of the Borough.[199] It was the culmination of an illustrious political career for Richard Corish, who had spent an entire lifetime serving the people of his beloved Wexford. Six months after his conferring he took ill, and following an operation at Wexford County Hospital, died on Thursday, 19 July 1945, aged just 58.

In his personal life, Richard met with Catherine Bergin, always called Katie, a seamstress/tailoress in Hadden's, North Main Street. They married on 29 September 1913. Corish was 26 years of age. Sometime following their marriage they moved into the house next door to 35 William Street, resulting in two Corish houses side by side.[200] Their first child, Richard (Dick), was born in August 1914, but died at a young age. Molly, their only daughter, was born in December 1915 and another son, Seán, in April 1917, followed by Brendan on 19 November 1918 and Fintan in July 1920. At this stage the house at William Street was overcrowded, so Richard and Catherine (Katie) moved to a newly built house at Number 1 St Ibar's Villas where their youngest son, Desmond, was born in November 1925. The Corish family had many happy memories of St Ibar's Villas, with the many dogs they had over the years and a rose garden and a patch for home-grown vegetables and tomato vines. The garden was a favourite spot for relaxation and for taking family photographs. Richard Corish had a workshop in the garden for his carpentry, skills he had learned from his father. Music played a big part in Richard's life, a love which passed down to his children later. The gramophone was in continuous use as the music of Strauss, Gilbert and Sullivan and John McCormack wafted in the air. His son, Brendan, appeared in *The Gondoliers* in 1938 and other productions with the Light Opera Society, Fintan played a role in *The Mikado* in 1942, while youngest son, Des, sang in *The Pirates of Penzance* and other productions. Richard's daughter, Mollie, also played leading roles with Wexford Light Opera Sociey and acted with the Wexford Theatre Guild. As Mayor of Wexford and president of Wexford Light Opera Society, Richard Corish introduced Ireland's tenor, John Count McCormack, at the Theatre Royal on the famous singer's farewell tour in 1940.[201]

Richard, Katie and Seán. (Courtesy of Helen Corish-Wylde)

After the death of Richard Corish, the sitting TD, it was necessary to call a by-election to fill the vacant Dáil seat, which was contested by his son Brendan. The 27-year-old Corish was born in Wexford on 19 November 1918. Educated locally at the Christian Brothers School, and amongst his youthful activities he was as a member of the 1st Wexford Scout Troop and played Gaelic football with John Street Volunteers. Aged 19 he joined the clerical staff of Wexford County Council. He was married to Phyllis Donahue and they had three sons: Richard, Philip and John.

In the 1945 Wexford by-election, Brendan Corish was elected to Dáil Éireann as a Labour Deputy on the opposition benches. Fianna Fáil had held power for a number of years at this time. In the general election of 1948, Corish held his seat as Fianna Fáil were returned to power once again as the largest party in Dáil Éireann. A coalition of Fine Gael, the Labour Party, the National Labour Party, Clann na Poblachta, Clann na Talmhan and a number of independent candidates came together to form the first inter-party government. Brendan Corish was appointed Parliamentary Secretary to the Minister for Defence and Local Government. In the following general election, in 1954, the second inter-party was formed and Corish was appointed Minister for Social Welfare.

Six years later, in 1960, Brendan Corish succeeded William Norton as Leader of the Labour Party. Introducing new policies which gave the party a more socialist outlook, the party moved very carefully as 'socialism' was still considered suspect in Ireland of the 1960s. Corish maintained that Ireland would be 'Socialist in the Seventies'. He was proven to be almost correct in his prediction when Fine Gael and the Labour Party formed a coalition government between 1973–7. Brendan Corish was second in command when he became Tánaiste and Minister for Health and Social Welfare. The Taoiseach at the time, Liam Cosgrave, called a general election in 1977. The government were defeated by Fianna Fáil, who returned to power following a landslide victory. Corish resigned as Leader of the Labour Party, having signalled his intention to do so before the election, and was succeeded as party leader by Frank Cluskey. Corish retired from politics completely at the February 1982 general election.[202]

Brendan Corish, MCC, was conferred with the Freedom of the Borough of Wexford in May 1984 in recognition of his political career and for his dedicated work on behalf of the poor, the old and the underprivileged. It was an historical occasion for the Corish family, as he was the second member in the same family to receive Wexford's highest honour.[203] Brendan Corish died on 17 February 1990 at the age of 71.

Desmond Corish (1925–2011) was the youngest son of Richard Corish. He was born on 28 November at St Ibar's Villas, Wexford, and was the brother of Brendan. Educated at Mercy Convent NS, Summerhill, Wexford, and at Christian Brothers Primary and Secondary Schools, Wexford, Des joined the staff of An Fóras Talúntais, Johnstown Castle as a laboratory assistant and later became a union official for the Irish Union of Distributive Workers and Clerks, Cavendish House, Parnell Square, Dublin. Returning to Wexford, he became a licensed vintner and proprietor of the Oak Lounge at 26 North Main Street, beside the Corish Memorial Hall where he became a union official for the Irish Transport and General Workers Union. Des was a Labour activist and lifelong socialist, and supported and helped his brother, Brendan, who became Labour TD for Wexford and Leader of the Labour Party as Tánaiste. In 1951, Des Corish served as Assistant National Organiser for the Labour Party and was a public representative for the Labour Party on Wexford Corporation and County Council. He was also Mayor of Wexford from 1973–4. He promoted environmental awareness and action and its links with tourism. His slogan was 'Keep Wexford Litter Free' and he encouraged the formation of residents' associations to improve and respect their areas for both residents and visitors alike. He championed the cause of the less well off in society and cared deeply about their working and living conditions. A committed Christian, he abhorred any form of social exclusion or bigotry. Des stood as a Labour Party candidate for the Wexford constituency in the 1982 general election.

Des Corish joined Wexford Light Opera Society in 1947, playing his first leading role in 1949 as Jack Point in *The Yeoman of the Guard*. Over the years he played many leading roles with the society, until his final appearance as Mr Murdock in *Brigadoon* in 1995. He was chairman of the society for many years and played a major part in the revival of Wexford Light Opera Society in 1964/65, and was an honorary life member for his outstanding contribution to the society. Des had many other interests including gardening, carpentry, local family history, wine making and travelling abroad with his wife on his retirement. Renowned for his sense of humour, he was a wonderful mimic and raconteur.

Des Corish married Eileen Meyler from Carrigeen Street, Wexford, in 1953. They had four children: Helen, Carmel, Peter and Des. Eileen predeceased Des in 2000.[204]

Des was the father of former Mayor of Wexford, Helen Corish-Wylde. Helen was born at St Therese's, Station Road, Rosslare Strand, Wexford, and was educated at Belgrove National School, Clontarf, Dublin. When the Corish family returned to live in Wexford, Helen continued her education at Presentation Sisters Convent schools at primary and secondary levels. She went on to teacher training at Carysfort College of Education, Blackrock, Co. Dublin, serving as a national school teacher from 1974–2009 at Convent of Mercy NS, St John's Road, Wexford town; Ballycanew NS, Gorey, Co. Wexford; and finally at Kennedy Park NS, Kennedy Park, Wexford town. While teaching in Kennedy Park NS she initiated the Green Schools Programme, as Green Schools coordinator and chairperson of the Green Committee. Kennedy Park NS was the first school in County Wexford to be awarded the prestigious Green Flag for Environmental Education, Awareness and Action in 2000.

Helen entered politics as a Labour Party candidate and was elected to Wexford Corporation in 1985, and served as Mayor of Wexford 1990–1. As a councillor, she represented Wexford Corporation on the national executive of Aontas, the umbrella organisation for adult education and lifelong learning where she was inspired by the vision, dedication and conviction of the members of the executive. As a committed socialist, Helen believed that equal opportunities for lifelong learning and second chance education for everyone were essential if inequality, depravation and social exclusion in our society were to be addressed.

She was elected as a councillor on Wexford County Council in 1991 as an independent candidate, and successfully campaigned for the very first arts officer to be appointed in County Wexford in 1993. Helen was confident that an arts officer would successfully promote Wexford town and county for all the arts, especially as the town of Wexford was already renowned for its annual Opera Festival founded in 1951. As a public representative, environmental awareness and action was high on Helen's agenda, and she promoted the responsibility of each individual within the local community to address environmental issues on a local, national and global basis. Helen Corish retired from politics in 1997.

In 1988, Helen founded, established and chaired 'Wexford in Bloom', an environmental organisation to hold an annual flower and environmental festival each July. The aim of this organisation was to have a litter-free Wexford town ablaze with colour from window boxes, hanging baskets adorning business premises and households throughout the town and its environs. Competitions were held during the flower festival which involved residents' groups, commercial and industrial sectors, schools and private gardens and other events to highlight the town for residents and tourists alike. In the first two years of the festival the committee sold 1,300 window boxes on a non-profit basis. Flowers beds were created in various urban areas with flowers and shrubs planted and tended regularly. Prior to this festival, window boxes were a rarity, and today it is heartening to view summer blooms spilling from window boxes throughout the town. 'Wexford in Bloom' promoted environmental awareness and action, and how to address the problem of global warming and climate change and the vital importance of recycling.

Helen is still involved in community projects and is chairperson of Wexford Memorial Trust Committee, responsible for the maintenance of Wexford's Paupers' Graveyard, and for organising an annual Patron ceremony. A former member of Wexford Light Opera Society and Wexford Drama Group, and with her vast local knowledge, Helen is a tour guide for Historical Walking Tours during Wexford Festival Opera. Her many and varied hobbies include playing the violin, reading, travelling in Ireland and abroad. Married to Donagh Wylde from Ennis, Co. Clare, a music teacher and choral director, the couple enjoy spending time with their two rescue dogs.[205]

Nicholas P. Corish, a first cousin of Richard Corish, was born in Cloughjordan, County Tipperary in 1897. He was one of the founding members of the Labour Party in Wexford. A schoolteacher by profession, he was responsible for establishing a branch of the Association of Secondary Teachers of Ireland (ASTI) in the town. He headed the poll in the local elections on no less than five occasions. An authority on the proportional representation system and the complexities involved in election counts, his work for the trade union movement in Wexford was widely recognised and his elevation to Life President of the Trades Council was a fitting tribute to the man and his endeavours. Alderman Corish was elected Mayor of Wexford in 1955. Following the Vatican Council, he played a role in Church affairs and was founder of the Invalid to Lourdes Association. His unselfishness involvement in Christian activities was rewarded when Pope John Paul II awarded him the Bene Merenti medal. He died on 17 April 1983.[206]

Philip Corish, son of Brendan Corish, began his interest in politics with his involvement in the fringes of election campaigns and began attending 'clinics' which his father, Brendan Corish, held throughout the county. He joined the Wexford town branch of the Labour Party, and when nominated as a delegate to the annual conferences the 1969 election, cemented his ambition to become more involved in politics. Philip took a high-level role in the 1973 election in Wexford, and he stood in the local elections in 1974 and headed the poll in the Wexford County Council area, and was the second elected candidate as an alderman to Wexford County Council. He was almost a full-time public representative at that time, his father being so busy with the affairs of government. Philip was his representative in the constituency and had an endless schedule of meetings, clinics and funerals.

Brendan Halligan, the General Secretary of the Labour Party and a friend of his father, advised Philip that he should gain some further academic qualifications. With this in mind, Philip entered and graduated from Trinity College, Dublin, with a degree in economics. He stood for re-election to Wexford County Council and Corporation in 1979, but failed in the former and his vote in the latter dropped considerably. Philip's father also stood for election and was easily elected to both bodies, with father and son attending a few Corporation meetings together. Philip gave a lot of deep thought to his situation during the summer of 1979, and opted to retire from the political scene altogether. He took a position with the Industrial Development Authority (IDA). Subsequent career opportunities with the IDA took Philip and his wife, Rosie, to Cork, New York and Los Angeles. In 1992, having left the IDA, Philip became an investment and small business consultant, managing development projects in Romania, Paraguay, Egypt, Lebanon, Jordan, Montenegro, Croatia, Ethiopia and Laos. Philip is now living in early retirement in France with his wife. Their two daughters have followed their careers in Dublin. Music and singing has always been part of Philip's life and he sang roles with his cousin, Helen, and uncle Des Corish in the Wexford Light Opera Society. He has maintained that interest and has performed with choirs all over the world and currently sings with three choirs in France. He owes that love of singing to Wexford Light Opera Society and its former musical director, Fr Johnny O'Brien.

From the election of Richard Corish to the Wexford Corporation in 1913, to the retirement from politics of his granddaughter, Helen Corish–Wylde in 1997, this Wexford family has made a massive contribution, at both local and national levels, to the political life of Wexford and Ireland for over eighty-four years of service.

SONGS OF THE WEXFORD COAST

Fr Joseph Ranson (1906–1964)

Situated on the east coast of Ireland, County Wexford has a long maritime history of ships, sailors and associations with the sea. The fishing industry prospered from the Hook to Rosslare to Poulshone near Courtown on the north of the coastline. Shipwrecks and sea disasters manifested themselves over the centuries, with the loss of hundreds of lives and many vessels on the hidden jagged rocks or marooned on shifting sandbanks. In his *Chronicles of the County Wexford*, George Griffiths lists no fewer than thirty-five shipwrecks over forty-five years from 1832 to 1877.[207] With so many disasters and shipwrecks, a catalogue of old sea ballads abounded in several pockets along the coast and its environs, commemorating a lot of the wrecks and rescues effected by the local people. In his enquiries in 1937 regarding the emigrant ship *Pomona* wrecked on the Blackwater Bank with the loss of 400 lives, Fr Joseph Ranson was directed to an elderly lady at Morriscastle. The 82-year-old, Margaret Mitten, had a wonderful store of memory and stanzas of old ballads and the lore of the Wexford coast just waiting to be discovered and collected. It was Margaret who introduced Fr Ranson to this wealth of song and other singers who also had the songs in their memories.

Following that first meeting with Margaret Mitten in Morriscastle,[208] the priest collected twelve songs in total, all transcribed by his sister-in-law, Miss Kathleen Hammel from Castle Annesley, Kilmuckridge. This was just the beginning for this clerical sea-song collector, as he discovered a whole fraternity of ballad singers around the coast. In turn, as songs were collected and noted down, each singer knew where the 'good songs' were to be heard and who sang them. A visit to John Mangan of Ballinahask, Kilmuckridge, had the words and air of 'The Poulshone Fishermen'. This ballad tells the story of four fishermen who sailed out on 3 April 1863 on a bright evening in near perfect conditions. A sudden squall capsized their yawl and pitched them overboard. A passing boat managed to save two of the four men and returned them to shore. The other two, Philip Leary and a man named Earle, were drowned. Their loss was lamented by parents and local people alike. The two survivors were Michael Redmond and Peter Kelly. Other ver-

Fr Joseph Ranson. (Painting by Colm Breen, Enniscorthy Museum)

sions and variants of this song were collected from Paddy Byrne, Killincooley; Jimmy Corrigan, Blackwater; and Tom Walsh, Curracloe. The air for this ballad was noted from the singing of Tom Walsh, Curracloe on 2 September 1946.[209] 'The Cumberland's Crew' was taken down from Phil Tobin of Curracloe, while another Curracloe man, Jack Golden, sang 'The Faythe Fishing Craft', which was allegedly composed by a Mr Twomey, a schoolteacher in Blackwater.[210] This song is written in 6/8 time and the notation is marked 'Brightly', and the opening stanza is couched in flowing language:

> The Faythe fishing craft on the twelfth of November,
> Their finny thread meshes they spread o'er the deep;
> Serene were the heavens, full well I remember,
> The wind in its cavern was buried in sleep.
> Tranquil the sea was, no greater our pleasure,
> save that of religion, blest heavenly treasure.
> Ere the mid time of night loudly roared beyond measure
> a tempest whose violence caused many to weep.

Their tale is told across eleven verses, naming the victims as Roche, Captain Rickards (Richards), Clarke, Brien and Campbell as described:

> They are gone; but enough, from your slumbers awaken,
> You minstrels of Erin, now chant their sad doom,
> Like five sturdy oaks by the rude storm shaken,
> Cut down neath the blast in perfection's full bloom.[211]

Fr Ranson had now donned the mantle of 'collector' of the ballads pertaining to the Wexford coast, and preserved the lyrics and most of the melodies to which these songs are sung. His contacts with the custodians of the ballads spread as he made acquaintances with these men and women. He endeavoured to make a complete collection of the sea ballads and had developed a chain of friends from Clone, south of the Arklow Rock, to Ballyhack in Waterford Harbour – all eager to help in the preservation of the ballads.

In his foreword to the collection, Fr Ranson suggests that the ballads should be sung very slowly. Jack Golden of Curracloe always referred to these songs of the sea as 'lamentations', and when the listener hears them sung to their plaintive airs it is easy to realise how right Jack Golden was. The singers Fr Ranson encountered were always anxious to acquire new songs and yet jealously guarded the ballads committed to memory in their own repertoire. For example, Jack Golden 'traded' 'The Faythe Fishing Craft' with a singer in Castletown[212] for the words of 'The Loss of the Atlantic', while Margaret Mitten paid for the song 'Paul Jones' by carrying twenty buckets of water to wet thatch for Johnny Sinnott of Morriscastle. Sinnott was very careful with his songs, rarely singing the same song twice in case some keen ear would pick it up. Having collected her many ballads, Margaret Mitten told Fr Ranson that she had some regret as she now had no song to sing when she would be taken to her final resting place in Donaghmore.[213] It was not unknown to have ballad singing contests to determine who the top ballad singer was by the number of songs he could sing. A challenge was issued by a singer from Ballygarret to a man named Redmond. The Ballygarret man stopped singing after sixty-three ballads, with Redmond singing his sixty-fourth, making him the winner. Jack Golden took part in a similar contest when he sang, song for song, for two sessions of six hours each against his opponent. With the new interest in ballad singing in Ireland, some songs from *Songs of the Wexford Coast* have come to the fore in singing clubs, namely: 'The Alfred D. Snow';[214] 'Bannow's Lonely Shore';[215] 'The Fethard Lifeboat Crew';[216] 'The Hantoon';[217] 'The Mexico';[218] 'The Pomona';[219] 'The Tinnaberna Fishermen' and several others from this collection. In the 1950s and '60s these songs were part of the repertoires of such notable Wexford ballad sing-ers as Jack Devereux and Elizabeth

Songs of the Wexford Coast cover.

Jefferies from Kilmore, Richard O'Neill from Enniscorthy, John Furlong from Tinnaberna and Leo Carthy from Carne, and in recent years the Berry brothers, Paddy and Phil and Phil's son, Ronán, sing the sea songs.

There are seventy-seven songs within Fr Ranson's *Songs of the Wexford Coast* collection, thirty-one of them with staff notation and others with the lyrics only. As already stated, the staff notation was transcribed by Miss Kathleen Hammel on location and the final editing of the melodies was by Miss Kathleen Grattan Flood. The notation for the printing blocks was prepared by Fr James Murphy, CC Enniscorthy. The collection was published by Fr. Ranson in 1948 and printed by Redmond Brothers, Enniscorthy. A reprint appeared in 1975 with an introduction by Fr James Hammel, nephew of the late Fr Ranson. The printers were John English and Co. Ltd, Wexford.

Fr Joseph Ranson was born in Kilmuckridge in 1906 and was the brother of Fr Robert Ranson, DD, and uncle of Fr James Hammel. Fr Ranson was educated at his local national school and CBS Gorey and St Peter's College, Wexford. He was ordained in 1930 at the Irish College, Salamanca, Spain. In 1949, he was appointed by the Bishops of Ireland as acting rector and archivist at the Irish College. He continued his work for four years at the Irish College, collating the manuscripts and contents of the archives, and organising their transfer to St Patrick's College, Maynooth. The Irish College and its associated properties then reverted to the Spanish State. His interest in the history and folklore of his native county inspired him and he served as Hon. Secretary of the Uí Cinsealaigh Historical Society in Enniscorthy for twenty years. He was editor of the society's journal, *The Past*, and was a member of the Royal Society of Antiquaries of Ireland. He founded the County Museum, which was housed in Enniscorthy Castle, purchased by the Athenaeum and opened at Eastertide 1962. As a priest, he ministered in various parishes throughout the Diocese of Ferns, and in October 1932 he was appointed curate in the Cathedral Parish, Enniscorthy, where most of his priestly life was spent. In failing health for some months, Fr Joseph Ranson died on 27 November 1964, aged 59 years.[220]

Fr Joseph Ranson had accomplished many things during his lifetime, and like Jacob Poole had the foresight to recognise the historical value of the sea ballads that would have been lost but for his diligence as a collector, culminating in his publication – *Songs of the Wexford Coast*.

Figurehead of *Pomona*. (Courtesy of Enniscorthy Museum, Gaul Collection)

~ 18 ~

WEXFORD FESTIVAL OPERA

Dr T.J. Walsh

On 21 October 1951, Wexford witnessed a veritable ongoing crescendo of opera and the arts with the founding of the Wexford Festival of Opera and the Arts. The phrase 'Ring up the curtain', of theatrical origin, certainly signified the beginning of a whole new era in the musical life of Wexford due to the monumental efforts of a team of opera buffs under the direction and leadership of Dr Thomas J. Walsh, a medical doctor in the small seaside town on the south-east coast of Ireland. The venue for the staging of 'live' opera was the Theatre Royal, situated on the High Street in the town. The venerable 'old lady' had witnessed many changes since the doors of the theatre were first opened in 1832.[221] Visiting touring opera companies such as Carl Rosa, Moody and Manners and Bowyer and Westwood played the Theatre Royal, presenting *Maritana*, *Bohemian Girl*, *Lily of Killarney*, *Rose of Castile*, *Il Trovatore* and many other works in the operatic repertoire. The theatre also served as a cinema following the removal of the galleries and boxes, and during the war years gradually began to fall into decay and disrepair. At one time the theatre was used to store furniture. However, a new day had dawned for the Theatre Royal with the Wexford Festival of Opera and the Arts.

Thomas J. Walsh was born in 1911 in Wexford town, elder son of John and Margaret Walsh. A younger brother, John, became a famous actor and television star, playing the role of Uncle James in *The Forsyth Saga* on BBC television. His only sister, Nellie Walsh, was the celebrated ballad singer and folk-song collector, and long-time compiler of the Songs and Cookery pages for *Ireland's Own* magazine. An extremely talented and artistic family, deeply involved in the choral and theatrical life of their small provincial Irish town. Tom Walsh always had an interest in music and singing, and had his first piano lessons from Miss Mary Codd, the church organist. Later in life, Tom Walsh had vocal training from the famous Italian singing teacher and musician, Maestro Adelio Viani, in Dublin in 1930.[222]

In 1950, Dr Walsh set up the Opera Study Circle in Wexford, which met at White's Hotel for evenings of listening to gramophone records and occasional lectures. For its inaugural meeting, Dr Tom had invited Sir Compton Mackenzie, then editor of *The Gramophone* magazine, to give a lecture to the society. At the close of the evening, Sir Compton suggested to Dr Walsh the idea of 'live on-stage' opera was not beyond the bounds of possibility and much better than listening to recordings of opera. What a great idea!

What did a hotelier, a postman and three medical doctors have in common? A love of opera. Dr Tom's past experience and expertise came to the fore once again, as the artistic director when the Wexford Festival of Opera and the Arts became a reality. The Theatre Royal was cleaned up and a veritable army of volunteer workers were recruited, with local craftsmen building the stage scenery and fitting up the antiquated lighting board. Advertising done, tickets on sale, rehearsals well in hand, the visiting principal stars contracted, a local chorus made up from church choirs, a male voice choir and other musical societies – it was almost time to 'Ring up the curtain'. Dr Walsh selected Balfe's *Rose of Castile*, one of the composer's lesser-performed works, and as a youth Balfe had spent some time in Wexford.[223] With house lights dimmed, Dermot O'Hara, conductor of the Radio Éireann Orchestra, made his entrance to a hushed auditorium. Baton raised, the overture played and the very first voice heard across the footlights was the rich contralto voice of Nellie Walsh. She sang the role of Louisa, an innkeeper. Wexford Festival of Opera and the Arts had begun.

Over the next fifteen years, Dr T.J. Walsh and his Festival Council presented no less than thirty operas covering Italian, French, German and two Irish composers, Michael William Balfe and Charles Villiers Stanford.

Singers made their operatic debuts and used Wexford Festival as a springboard to other opera houses. One of the most famous singers to come to Wexford was Mirella Freni. Production of the lesser-known operas brought impresarios to Wexford to view these works for the first time in the pocket-sized theatre in the High Street. Dr Walsh and his Opera Festival were a major force in the operatic world, and soon ranked with Bayreuth, Salzburg, Glyndebourne and Aldeburgh Festivals. Recitals were an integral part of the festival, with such luminaries as pianists Julius Katchen, Paul Badura-Skoda and Rosalyn Tureck, woodwind players such as Leon Goosens and Elaine Shaffer, violinist Alfredo Campoli and guitarist Andres Segovia. Orchestras such as the BBC Symphony and the Halle with Sir John Barbirolli took part. In those halcyon years of the Wexford Festival, admission prices for recitals ranged from 10/6, 7/6 and 5/-, with admission to the operatic dress rehearsals at 5/-.

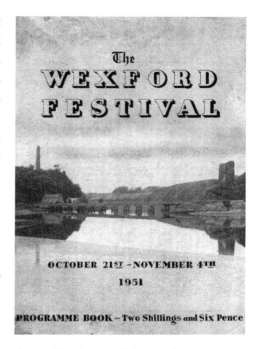

Cover of the first Wexford Festival programme.

Many honours were bestowed on Dr Walsh, including an honorary PhD and DLitt from UCD and a Fellowship of the Royal Historical Society. He was also a Knight of Malta and a Freeman of the Town of Wexford. A series of scholarly publications and books on the history of opera came from the pen of Dr Walsh as he left his mark in the literary world.[224] Little did he think that the Festival of Opera and the Arts that he started in 1951 would still be going strong many decades later, in the National Opera House built on the site of the Theatre Royal where it all began. Dr T.J. Walsh died on 8 November 1988, and is buried in the family plot in St Alphonsus Church Cemetery, Barntown, County Wexford.

Wexford Festival

OPERA

"THE ROSE OF CASTILE"

(M. W. BALFE)

THEATRE ROYAL, WEXFORD

8.15 p.m.

NOVEMBER 1st (Gala Performance), 2nd, 3rd and 4th

MAUREEN SPRINGER   MURRAY DICKIE

COLORATURA SOPRANO,   TENOR,

of Glyndebourne Opera and Edinburgh Festival   of Covent Garden and Teatro dell' Opera, Rome

STATIA KEYES   NELLIE WALSH

JAMES BROWNE   JAMES G. CUTHBERT   MICHAEL HANLON

Prima Ballerina—JOAN DENISE MORIARTY.

Settings by MICHAEL O'HERLIHY.

FESTIVAL CHORUS AND RADIO EIREANN LIGHT ORCHESTRA

CONDUCTOR — # DERMOT O'HARA

Admission—10/6, 7/6, 5/-, 3/6. Booking at Theatre Royal daily from Thurs., Oct. 25th, 2.30 to 5.30. Sun. 10.30 to 1 p.m.

RECITALS

THE WORLD FAMOUS PIANIST,

WEINGARTEN

TECHNICAL SCHOOL—NOV. 4th at 3.30 p.m.—ADMISSION 5/-

THE CELEBRATED VIOLINIST,

JAROSLAV VANECEK

Accompanist—KITTY O'CALLAGHAN

TECHNICAL SCHOOL—NOV. 1st at 3.30 p.m.—ADMISSION 5/-

GRAND FINALE OF FESTIVAL

COSTUME BALL

TOWN HALL, TUESDAY 6th NOVEMBER 7.45 p.m.   ADMISSION 3/6

Poster of events, Wexford Festival 1951.

⌐ 19 ⌐

A HURLING HERO

Nickey Rackard

The great sports commentator Micheál O'Hehir[225] summed up the hurling prowess and physical strength of Nickey Rackard, the Wexford Senior Hurling team's full-forward, when he described the taking of a 21-yard free by the 6ft 2in blond colossus as follows: 'He bends, he lifts and he strikes! It's a goal – another Rackard Special!' Many spectators would never forget the goal machine that crashed through the stoutest and biggest defences and delivered a coup de grace with thunderous shooting that tore the goal nets from their rigging.[226]

Nickey Rackard was born on 28 April 1922 in Killanne, County Wexford, the eldest son in a family of five boys and four girls. The girls were Sally, Essie, Molly and Rita, and Nickey's brothers were Jim, Bobby, John and Billy. Their mother was Anastasia Doran from the nearby parish of Davidstown, where Robert Rackard and her married in 1918. The Rackard children were all very tall, a trait they most likely inherited from their mother Anastasia. She was a tall, elegant woman herself. The Rackards were farmers with sheep and dairy cows, and they also kept horses. The children worked hard on the family farm, tending to the various chores such as dipping the sheep, helping in the dairy with the separation of the milk and the many other tasks to be attended to on a farm. Their father had a great knowledge of horses and passed this on to the children, all of whom were proficient horse riders at a young age. In his later years, Nickey often reflected on the happy and pleasant childhood days growing up in Killanne, situated beneath the Blackstairs

Mountains, and their farm with its animal stock, stores and barns and the shop, grocery and public house under the watchful eye of Mrs Rackard.[227]

Robert and Anastasia had just a passing interest in sport, and Nickey's father had expected his eldest boy would play cricket. How wrong he was, for the young Rackard was much more interested in Gaelic games. Having finished his early education at the local school, Nickey went on to St Kieran's College, Kilkenny, where hurling was high on the agenda for college sporting activities. Going on to University College Dublin, Rackard studied to be a veterinary surgeon. On the sporting field he played his club hurling with Rathnure, enjoying great success. In 1948 he won his first county title with the club, and two years later, in 1950, he won his second county title, giving him the opportunity to take over the role of captain of the county senior team the following year. He won his third county medal in 1955.

Playing in the forward lines, he won his first Leinster Championship medal in 1951 and Wexford faced Tipperary in the All-Ireland final. Tipperary were attempting to win their three-in-a-row titles, and the Munster men ran riot with a final score of 7 goals 7 points to 3 goals 9 points. Having lost their Leinster crown in 1952, Wexford regained the title in 1954, defeating Dublin when Rackard scored 5 goals and 5 points from Wexford's total score of 8–5. Having defeated Antrim, Wexford faced Cork in the struggle

Nickey Rackard at Croke Park.

for All-Ireland honours. A huge crowd filled Croke Park to witness the expected struggle between Rackard and Christy Ring,[228] especially as Cork were chasing a three-in-a-row victory. Cork succeeded in their quest, defeating Wexford with a score line of 1–9 to 1–6. Rackard won his third Leinster title in 1955 and Wexford went on to defeat Limerick in the All-Ireland semi-final, and in September of that year they faced Galway in the deciding game of the championship. Fortune smiled on the Slaneysiders[229] when a goal by Tim Flood in the final nine minutes gave Wexford a 3–13 to 2–8 win. It was Wexford's first championship since 1910,[230] and Nickey Rackard added an All-Ireland medal to his collection. The following year, Wexford won their first National Hurling League title and went on to win the Leinster title, giving Rackard his fourth Leinster medal. The All-Ireland final was contested between Wexford and Cork, with the Wexford men aiming to retain their title and to gain revenge over Cork for the defeat of 1954. According to the pundits, this game has gone down in the annals of hurling as one of the all-time classics. Christy Ring was bidding for his ninth All-Ireland, and a miraculous save by goalkeeper Art Foley from a Ring shot turned the game in Wexford's favour. Foley cleared the ball up the field to set up another Wexford attack. Rackard scored a crucial goal in the final two minutes of the game, giving Wexford a 2–14 to 2–8 victory over the Leesiders.[231] Following a defeat in the Leinster final of 1957, Nickey Rackard decided to retire from inter-county hurling. There were various attempts to persuade him to reconsider his retirement, in particular from full-back Nick O'Donnell, who expressed his personal dissatisfaction to Rackard. O'Donnell told him that he should have played on. Nickey Rackard made the following statement to GAA journalist , Mick Dunne: 'I'll be 36 next April; there's no use prolonging it. The way I look at it is the sooner I go, then the sooner Wexford will be able to get a replacement and begin to build a team for next year.'

Nickey Rackard played his final game of hurling at the end of September 1957. It was the Wexford County final between Rathnure, Nickey's club team, and St Aidan's. Luck was not to grace the hurling giant's final game, for his team were beaten by 5 goals and 10 points to 2 goals and 5 points.[232]

The gentle giant from Killanne experienced a troubled life away from the sporting field, resulting in his dependency on alcohol. He finally joined AA[233] and gradually pieced his life together, rebuilding his veterinary practice. Following a battle with cancer, Nickey Rackard died at St Vincent's Hospital, Dublin, on 10 April 1976, aged 53.

On Monday, 19 March 2012, the citizens of Wexford witnessed the unveiling of a new work of street sculpture in the form of a magnificent bronze statue of County Wexford's hurling hero, Nickey Rackard. The life-sized statue, the work of sculptor Mark Richards, stands in Selskar Square and was commissioned and erected by Wexford Borough Council. The ceremony was attended by a large group of people including the Bishop of Ferns, Rev.

Billy, Nickey and Bobby. (Courtesy of Denis O'Connor Archive)

Denis Brennan, who blessed the statue. Also present were members of Wexford Borough Council and Councillor David Hynes, Mayor of Wexford, who unveiled the statue to the delight and prolonged applause of all. It's interesting to note that the stonework of the plinth and placing of the bronze sculpture was carried out by Martin Codd, son of Martin Codd, a teammate of Nickey Rackard on the victorious Wexford hurling team of 1955 and 1956. Also present was the late Tom Williams, author of the song 'Cuchulainn's Son' which has now become an anthem for all followers of Wexford Gaelic games. Some phrases from Tom's lyric are carved on three sides of the plinth. Nickey Rackard's son, Bobby, spoke of the pride his father would have felt to see his statue sited in the heart of Wexford town, the capital of County Wexford. He was always an extremely proud Wexford man.

Nickey Rackard, bronze; Selskar, Wexford. (Gaul Collection)

Nickey Rackard is regarded as one of the greatest hurlers of all time. He was also on a list of top-scoring greats, having notched up a total of 59 goals and 96 points during his hurling career. The story of the 6ft 2in hurling hero was recounted in a biography of Rackard by Wexford author Tom Williams.[234] in his book entitled *Cuchulainn's Son – The Story of Nickey Rackard*. Some lines from Tom Williams' song remind us of the talent of the great Nickey Rackard:

The challenge of an ancient game
Brought glory, glory to your name,
Though March winds blew the crowds still came,
To watch you gentle hero.

We watched you on September fields,
And lightning was the drive,
You were the one Cuchulainn's Son in 1955.

BIBLIOGRAPHY

A Century of Progress, 1839–1939, Browne and Nolan, Dublin 1939

Bassett, George Henry, *Wexford Borough and County Guide and Directory*, Dublin 1885

Berry, Paddy, *Kilmachree, A simple history of Kilmachree Parish,* Wexford 2015

Bierney, Rev. M. (ed.) *The Centenary Record of Wexford's Twin Churches 1858–1958*, Wexford 1958

Boylan, Henry, *A Dictionary of Irish Biography*, Dublin 1978

Browne, Bernard, *Living by the Pen*, Wexford 1997

Carolan, Ns., *A Harvest Saved, Francis O'Neill and Irish Music in Chicago*, Cork 1997

Cowley, R., Parker, G. (ed.), *The Reader's Companion to Military History*, USA 1996

Dearmer, P., Shaw, M., Williams, R.V. (ed.), *The Oxford Book of Carols*, London 1928

Debrett's Illustrated Peerage of the United Kingdom of Great Britain and Ireland, 1865

Delaney, James G., 'Patrick Kennedy, folklorist', *The Past*, No. 14, 1983

Dolan, T. P., Ó Muirithe, Dr D., *The Dialect of Forth and Bargy*, Dublin 1996

Doyle, Eamon, *Tales of the Anvil*, Nonsuch, Dublin 2008

Duffy, John, *River Slaney from source to sea*, Tullow, Carlow 2006

Dunlop, A., *The Life of Vice-Adm. Sir Robt. John Le Mesurier McClure*, Rhodesia 1975

Enright, Michael, *Men of Iron*, Wexford Foundry Disputes, Wexford 1987

Fleischmann, Aloys, (ed.) *Music in Ireland*, Cork 1952

Flood, David, 'The Ancient Order of Foresters', *Irish Times*, July 2017

Flood, Wm. Henry Grattan, *The Story of the Bagpipe*, London 1911

Flood, Wm. Henry Grattan, *A History of Irish Music*, Dublin 1905

Flood, Wm. Henry Grattan, *The Story of the Harp*, London 1905

Frost, John, *American Naval Biography*, USA

Gahan, Daniel, *The People's Rising, Wexford 1798*, Dublin 1998

Gahan, John V., *The Secular Priests of the Diocese of Ferns*, Strasbourg 2000

Gaul, Liam, *Masters of Irish Music*, Nonsuch, Dublin 2006

Gaul, Liam, 'John and James Cash, pipers', *Kilmore Parish Journal*, No. 38, 2010

Gaul, Liam, *A Window on the Past,* self -published, Wexford 2012

Gaul, Liam, *Wexford – the American Connection*, Wexford Borough Council, Wexford 2013

Gaul, Liam, *Johnstown Castle – A History*, Dublin 2014

Goff, Jennifer, *Eileen Gray, Her Work and Her World*, Sallins, Co. Kildare 2015

Griffiths, George, *The Chronicles of the County Wexford*, Enniscorthy 1890

Halligan, Brendan, *Brendan Corish, a tribute*, Scáthán Press, Dublin

Hurley-Binions, G., *1798–1998 – Killanne Rathnure, A Local History*, Enniscorthy 1997

Jeffrey, W.H., *The Castles of Co. Wexford*, Private Publication, Wexford 1979

Kavanagh, A., Murphy. R., *The Wexford Gentry Vol. 1*, Co. Wexford 1994

Kavanagh, A., Murphy. R., *The Wexford Gentry Vol. 2*, Co. Wexford 1994

Kehoe, Mary T., *Wexford Town – its streets and people*, Wexford 1980

Kelly, Ronan, *Bard of Erin, The Life of Thomas Moore*, Dublin 2008

Kennedy, Patrick, *Evenings in the Duffry (1875),* reprint Kessinger Publishing, USA

Kennedy, Patrick, *Legends of Mount Leinster*, Duffry Press, Enniscorthy 1989

Kennedy, Patrick, *The Banks of the Boro*, Duffry Press, Enniscorthy 1989

Kinsella, Anna, *Women of Wexford 1798–1998*, Dublin 1998

Lewis, Kevin, *What the Doctor Ordered*, Nonsuch, Dublin 2008

MacLysaght, Edward, *More Irish Families*, Irish Academic Press, Dublin 1982

McClure, J.A., *The McClure Family*, Petersburg, Virginia, USA 1914

McGrath, Tim, *John Barry, An American Hero in the Age of Sail*, USA 2011

McMahon, S., O'Donoghue, J. (ed.), *Brewers Dictionary of Irish Phrase and Fable*, London 2004

McNamara, Sarah, *Those Intrepid United Irishwomen*, Limerick 1995

Madders, Ambrose, *'98 Diary, Ireland in Rebellion*, Wexford 1997

Meleady, Dermot, 'John Redmond – Parnellite and Nationalist', *Journal of Wexford Historical Society*, No. 21, 2006–07

Meleady, Dermot, *John Redmond, The National Leader*, Dublin 2014

Mitchell, Pat, *The Dance Music of Willie Clancy*, Dublin and Cork 1976

Moore, Norman, 'Jacob Poole', *Dictionary of National Biography*, 1885–1900, Vol. 46

Murphy, Celestine (ed.), *Wexford Connections, the Redmond Family and National Politics,* Wexford Co. Council Library Service, 2018

Murphy, Hilary, *Families of County Wexford*, Wexford 1986

Murphy, Hilary, 'Pierces of the Foundry', *Kilmore Parish Journal*, No. 18, 1989–90

O'Byrne, Rev. S. (ed.), *The College Hymnal*, John English & Co. Ltd, Wexford 1964

Ó Broin, Gearóid, 'Jacob Poole of Growtown', *Journal of the Taghmon Historical Society*, Vol. 3, 1999

Ó Faoláin, Seán, *With the Gaels of Wexford*, Enniscorthy 1955

O'Neill, Capt. Francis, *Irish Folk Music, A Fascinating Hobby*, Chicago 1910

O'Neill, Capt. Francis, *Irish Minstrels and Musicians*, Chicago 1913

O'Sullivan, Dr A.M., 'Pierces of Wexford', *Journal of Wexford Historical Society*, No. 16

Osborn, Capt. Sherard (ed.), *The Discovery of the North-West Passage*, London 1857

Poole, Jacob, *A Glossary of the Old Dialect of the English Colony in the Baronies of Forth and Bargy*, (ed.) Rev. Wm Barnes, London 1867

Rackard, Billy, *No Hurling at the Dairy Door*, Blackwater Press, Dublin 1996

Rafferty, Celestine (ed.), *Between Place and Parish,* Wexford Co. Library Service, 2004

Rafferty, C., 'Mr. Pierce of Tenacre', *The Twin Churches Book 1858–2008*, Wexford

Ranson, Fr Joseph, *Songs of the Wexford Coast*, Enniscorthy 1948

Reck, Padge, *Wexford – A Municipal History*, Mulgannon Pubs, Wexford 1987

Redmond, Louis (ed.), *Modern Irish Lives*, Dublin 1996

Roche, Kieran S., *Richard Corish, A Biography*, Original Writing, Dublin 2012

Roche, W., Rossiter, N., Hurley, K., Hayes, T., *Walk Wexford Ways*, Wexford 1988, p. 29

Rossiter, Nicky, *Main Street – Heart of Wexford*, The History Press Ireland, Dublin 2018

Rowe, David, Scallan, Eithne, *Houses of Wexford* (2nd edition), Clare 2016

Ruddock, Rev. N., Kloss, N., *Unending Worship*, Wexford 1997

Ryan, Liam, *The Awful Tragedy of the Helen Blake Lifeboat, Fethard, Co. Wexford 1914*, New Ross, Co. Wexford 2010

Scallan, Eithne, *The Twin Churches Book 1858–2008*, Wexford 2008

Tóibín, Colm, Rafferty, Celestine (ed.), *Enniscorthy – A History*, Enniscorthy 2000

Vallely, Fintan (ed.), *The Companion to Irish Traditional Music*, C.U.P., Cork 1999

Vignoles, O.J., *Brief Sketch of the Career of Sir Robt. P. Stewart*, London 1897–98

Wallace, Martin, *100 Irish Lives*, David & Charles, London 1983

Walsh, Dan, *Bree – The Story of a County Wexford Parish*, Enniscorthy 1980

Walsh, Dan, *100 Country Houses*, Enniscorthy 1996

Walsh, Dr T.J., *Opera in Old Dublin 1819–1838*, Free Press, Wexford 1952

Walsh, Dr T.J., *Opera in Dublin 1705–1797*, Allen Figgis, Dublin 1973

Walsh, Dr T.J., *Monte Carlo Opera 1879–1909*, Gill & Macmillan, Dublin 1975

Williams, Tom, 'Canon Jas. Roche – Fundraiser Supreme, Last Parish Priest of Wexford', *The Twin Churches Book 1858–2008*, (ed.) Eithne Scallan, Wexford 2008

Williams, Tom, *Cúchulainn's Son, The Story of Nickey Rackard*, Dublin 2006

102 Years of Wexford I.C.A., Wexford 2000, Enniscorthy 2012

NEWSPAPERS

Dungarvan Leader and Southern Democrat, 1945

Enniscorthy Echo, 1934

The People, 1918, 1934

The Irish Times, 2017, 2018

Wexford Independent, 1851, 1853, 1855, 1868

The Daily Telegraph, 2009

JOURNALS

Kilmore Parish Journal, Nos. 18 and 38
Wexford Historical Society, No. 16
The Musical Times, Vol. 69, No. 1027
The Past, No. 14
Taghmon Historical Society, Vol. 3, 1999
The Other Clare, Vol. 33

WEBSITES

cyberboxingzone.com/boxing/roche-jem.htm
www.irishtimes.com/wexford-footballers-have-had-a-few-jems-down-the-years
www.rte.ie/..../radio-documentary-richard-croker-ireland-tammany-hall-new-york.
  htm
www.librarything.com/profile/georgepreble
www. libraryireland.com/biography/MylesByrne.php
www.britannica.com/technology.com/technology/dead-reckoning.navigation
www.ushistory.org/valleyforge/served/cadwaladar.html
www.history.com/topics/american-revolution/battles-of-trenton-and-princeton
www.history.com/topics/us-presidents/george-washington
www.rmg.co.uk/discover/robert-mcclure-north-west-passage-expedition-1850
https://comhaltas.ie/blog/past/history-of-the-pipers-club
www.sligotowncce.com/fodwinners.html
https://en.wikipedia.org/wiki/seán-potts
https://stairnaheireann.net/2013/11/19-1918-labour-party-leader-brendan-corish/
rte.ie/archives/exhibitions/1411-radio-sports.../1452-michael-ohehir/
www.rmg.co.uk/discover/explore/robert-mcclure-north-west-passage-ex-
  pedition-1850
www.independent.ie/life/home-garden/interiors/98-facts-about-eileen-gray
https://www.independent.ie/lifestyle/visionary-gray-shines-strong-29135137.html
www.nytimes.com/2001/07/20/arts/art-in-review-wendingen-dutch-design

ENDNOTES

1   *American Naval Biography comprising Lives of the Commodores and other Commanders distinguished in The History of the American Navy*, John Frost, p. 75.

2   Tacumshin is a small village in the south-east of County Wexford, Ireland. It is located 15km south of Wexford town. Historians believe that John Barry was born at Ballysampson near the village. *Wexford – the American Connection*, Liam Gaul, p.41.

3   George Henry Preble was born in 1816. He retired at the rank of rear admiral in 1878 and devoted himself to naval history. He died in Brookline, Mass., on 1 March 1885. www.librarything.com/profile/george preble.

4   Dead reckoning, determination without the aid of celestial navigation of the position of a ship or aircraft from the record of the courses sailed or flown, the distance made (which can be estimated from velocity), the known starting point, and the known or estimated drift. www.britannica.com/technology/dead-reckoning-navigation.

5   John Cadwalader was born in Pennsylvania in 1742. He was involved in Washington's plan for attack on Trenton in 1776. However, he and his men were unable to cross the Delaware south of Trenton in sufficient strength to be of any real aid. Washington himself admired and even coveted Cadwalader's abilities. By the autumn of 1777, Washington requested Cadwalader to organise militia on the Maryland eastern shore. He did see action at Brandywine and Germantown, as well as volunteering after Valley Forge at Monmouth. On 4 July 1778, Cadwalader fought a duel with Thomas Conway. He shot him in the mouth. Following the war, he moved from Philadelphia to Maryland. He became a state legislator. He died at the age of 43 in 1786. www.ushistory.org/valleyforge/served/cadwalader.html.

6   The Battle of Trenton. The Hessian force at Trenton numbered 1,400 under the leadership of Colonel Johann Rall. Although Rall had received warnings of colonial movements, his men were exhausted and unprepared for Washington's attack. As he approached the town, Washington divided his men, sending flanking columns under General Nathaniel Greene and General John Sullivan. Meanwhile, Colonel Henry Knox's cannons fired on the garrison. Rall attempted to rally his troops but was never able to establish a defensive perimeter, and was shot from his horse and fatally wounded. The Hessians quickly surrendered. www.history.com/topics/american-revolution/battles-of-trenton-and-princeton.

7   The Battle of Princeton. Realising his men could not hold Trenton, Washington withdrew across the Delaware. On 30 December he crossed back into New Jersey with an army of 2,000, informed that 8,000 British troops under Generals Charles Cornwallis and James Grant were marching south from Princeton. On New Year's Day, Washington's force of 5,000 poorly trained men massed in Trenton. The next day Cornwallis arrived with an army of 5,500. After skirmishes at the American lines and three attempts to cross the bridge at Assunpink Creek, Cornwallis relented for the day. That night, Washington deployed 500 men to keep the campfires going while the rest of his troops made a night-time march north to Princeton. At dawn on 3 January 1777, Cornwallis woke to find that his opponent had disappeared, while Washington's men were nearing the end of their 12-mile march to Princeton. Washington sent a small force under General Hugh Mercer to destroy a bridge. Mercer's men encountered Redcoats and Mercer was killed in the fighting. Arriving militiamen under Col Cadwalader had little effect. Then Washington arrived, riding between the firing lines until his terrified horse refused to go on. The Americans rallied and broke through Mercer's lines. As at Trenton, the Americans quickly withdrew after winning the Battle of Princeton. Washington's men marched to Morristown, in northern New Jersey, where they established winter quarters, safe from British incursions. The Continental Army basked in its achievements – at Princeton they had defeated a regular British Army in the field. Washington had shown that he could unite soldiers from all the colonies into an effective national force. www.history.com/topics/american-revolution/battles-of-trenton-and-princeton

8   Charles Cornwallis led several successful early campaigns during the American Revolution, securing British victories at New York, Brandywine and Camden. In 1781, as second in command to Gen. Henry Clinton, he moved his forces to Virginia, where he was defeated at the Battle of Yorktown. This American victory was the final major conflict of the American Revolution. Charles Cornwallis saw military service in Germany during the Seven Years' War, fighting at Minden (1759). He became major general in 1775.

As Lord Lieutenant and Commander-in-Chief of Ireland, Cornwallis unsuccessfully argued for Catholic emancipation, and helped secure passage of the Act of Union, which created the United Kingdom of Great Britain and Ireland. As Commander-in-Chief and Governor General of Ireland (1797–1801), Cornwallis defeated the Irish rebellion and the limited French invasion of 1798. *The Reader's Companion to Military History*, edited by Robert Cowley and Geoffrey Parker, Houghton Mifflin Harcourt Publishing Company, USA 1996, p.109.

9 George Washington (1732–99) was Commander-in-Chief of the Continental Army during the American Revolutionary War (1775–83) and served two terms as the first US President, from 1789 to 1797. Washington was raised in colonial Virginia. During the American Revolution, he led the colonial forces to victory over the British and became a national hero. In 1787, he was elected president of the convention that wrote the US Constitution. Two years later, Washington became America's first president. As president, he handed down a legacy of strength, integrity and national purpose. Shortly after leaving office, he died at his Virginia plantation, Mount Vernon, at age 67. Known as the 'Father of His Country', his face appears on the US dollar bill and quarter, and hundreds of US schools and towns, as well as the nation's capital city, are named for him. www. history.com/topics/us-presidents/george-washington

10 *Tim McGrath and John Barry, An American Hero in the Age of Sail*, Westholme Publishing, Yardley, Pennsylvania, 2011, pp. 353–54; 405; 409–410.

11 'Jacob Poole', Norman Moore, *Dictionary of National Biography 1885–1900*, Vol. 46.

12 'Jacob Poole of Growtown – and the Yola Dialect', Gearóid Ó Broin, *Journal of the Taghmon Historical Society*, Vol. 3, 1999, pp. 42–9.

13 In the Preface to the 1979 Edition of *The Dialect of Forth and Bargy Co. Wexford, Ireland*, (ed.) T.P. Dolan and Diarmaid Ó Muirithe, the authors state that the manuscript edited by the Rev. William Barnes was faulty in many respects. His etymologies are untrustworthy and for that reason mainly, the present writers have attempted the task of re-editing Jacob Poole's manuscripts. Also included are words incorporated by Barnes from Stanyhurst's 'Notice of Wexford' in *Holinshed's Chronicles* and words that General Vallency claimed to have collected from an 'old gentleman named Browne' but in reality, according to Poole's family, filched from him by the general and published, without permission, in the *Transactions of the Royal Irish Academy* in 1788. In crediting the general with these words, the present editors are giving him the benefit of the doubt. *The Dialect of Forth and Bargy Co. Wexford, Ireland*, (ed.) T.P. Dolan and Diarmaid Ó Muirithe, Four Courts Press, Dublin, 1996, p. 7.

14   'Jacob Poole', Norman Moore, *Dictionary of National Biography 1885–1900*, Vol. 46.

15   *Kilmachree, a simple history of Kilmachree Parish*, compiled and written by Paddy Berry, Wexford, 2015, pp. 18–9.

16   'Jacob Poole of Growtown – and the Yola Dialect', Gearóid Ó Broin, *Journal of the Taghmon Historical Society*, Vol. 3, 1999, pp.42–9.

17   *The Dialect of Forth and Bargy Co. Wexford, Ireland*, (ed.) T.P. Dolan and Diarmaid Ó Muirithe, pp.12–3.

18   *ibid*. p.13.

19   *A Glossary of the Old Dialect of the English Colony in the Baronies of Forth and Bargy*, Jacob Poole, (ed.) William Barnes, B.D., London, 1867, p. 111.

20   *ibid*. pp. 102–3.

21   *ibid*. pp. 84–91; 93–101; 106–9.

22   'Jacob Poole', Norman Moore, *Dictionary of National Biography 1885–1900*, Vol. 46.

23   'Jacob Poole of Growtown – and the Yola Dialect', Gearóid Ó Broin, *Journal of The Taghmon Historical Society*, Vol. 3, 1999, p. 48.

24   *The Dialect of Forth and Bargy Co. Wexford, Ireland*, (ed.) T.P. Dolan and Diarmaid Ó Muirithe, p. 13.

25   The Cornmarket is situated close to the former site of St John's Gate, one of the entrance gates to the walled town. Rural people entered through this gate and set up their stalls in Cornmarket to sell their produce. The Market House, later known as the Assembly Rooms, was built in 1775. It has a beautiful Georgian ceiling and five crystal chandeliers in the ballroom. Off the ballroom was the Supper Room. The ceiling with its ornate plasterwork still survives. *Wexford Town – its streets and people*, Mary T. Kehoe c. 1980, p. 23.

26   Kelly, Ronan, *Bard of Erin, The Life of Thomas Moore*, Penguin Ireland, Dublin 2008, p. 14.

27   Edward Bunting (1773–1843). Born in Armagh. Played the organ at St Anne's Church, Belfast. In 1792, the 19-year-old Bunting was commissioned to write down in staff notation the tunes played by the eleven harpers participating in the Belfast Harp Festival. His collections preserved many of our most beautiful melodies from oblivion. His first publication in 1796 contained

66 tunes, his second in 1809 of seventy-seven melodies, with his third and final publication in 1840 of 151 tunes. Soon after his final publication, Edward Bunting took ill and died suddenly on 21 December 1843. He is buried in Mount Jerome Cemetery, Dublin. *Masters of Irish Music*, Liam Gaul. Nonsuch Publishing Ltd, Dublin 2006, pp. 15–7.

28   Kelly, Ronan, *Bard of Erin, The Life of Thomas Moore*, Penguin Ireland, Dublin 2008, pp. 524–5.

29   Hedge schools were the paying schools during the eighteenth and early nineteenth centuries and were conducted in sheds, barns or hovels or in the shelter of a hedge in summertime. Catholic schools were prohibited by the Popery Laws and a schoolmaster could be punished by transportation. Such schools were hidden away for fear of detection by the authorities. Pupils of all ages were in the same class with varied curricula which included Latin and Greek. The pupils' parents paid the schoolmaster a small fee in coin or in kind. In 1824, it is estimated that 9,000 such schools were in operation, with 300,000–400,000 children attending from the 1820s. Catholic emancipation and the emergence of the first national schools brought about the end of the hedge schools. *Brewers Dictionary of Irish Phrase and Fable* (ed. S. McMahon and J.O'Donoghue) London 2004, p. 365.

30   *The Secular Priests of the Diocese of Ferns*, John V. Gahan, Strasbourg, Cedex 2, France, 2000. p. 248.

31   *ibid*. pp.166–7.

32   Monday, 21 May, Lord Edward Fitzgerald was arrested in the evening. He was badly wounded in the ensuing scuffle. *'98 Diary, Ireland in Rebellion*, Ambrose Madders, Wexford 1997, p. 15.

33   On Wednesday, 23 May, the date of the rising, Anthony Perry was arrested and tortured in Gorey by the North Cork Militia. Perry was pitch capped and was forced to reveal the names of all the principal leaders of the United Irishmen in Wexford/South Wicklow. *'98 Diary, Ireland in Rebellion*, Ambrose Madders, Wexford 1997, p. 15.

34   *ibid*. p. 19.

35   *ibid*. p. 23.

36   *The Wexford Gentry Vol. II*, Art Kavanagh and Rory Murphy, Bunclody, Co. Wexford, p. 102.

37   *'98 Diary, Ireland in Rebellion*, Ambrose Madders, Wexford 1997, pp. 26–7.

38   All historical facts and accounts of the insurrection in County Wexford in 1798 were gleaned from the following works: *The People's Rising, Wexford 1798*, Daniel Gahan, Dublin, 1995; *'98 Diary, Ireland in Rebellion*, Ambrose Madders, Wexford 1997; *Brewers Dictionary of Irish Phrase and Fable* (ed. S. McMahon and J.O'Donoghue) London 2004; http://www.libraryireland.com/biography/MylesByrne.php

39   All historical facts and accounts of John Kelly were gleaned from *John Kelly of Killanne 1798–1998, Killanne-Rathnure*, a local history compiled by Gloria Hurley-Binions, Enniscorthy 1997, pp. 1–17.

40   'Patrick Kennedy, folklorist', James G. Delaney, *The Past*, No. 14, 1983, pp. 49–66.

41   *ibid*. p. 51.

42   *ibid*. p. 51.

43   *ibid*. pp. 53–4.

44   *ibid*. p. 54.

45   *Living by the Pen*, Bernard Browne, Wexford 1997, pp. 81–2.

46   *Evenings in the Duffry* was published by Kessinger Publishing, USA.

47   Two of these rare books have been reprinted and published by Duffry Press, Court Street, Enniscorthy.

48   'Patrick Kennedy, folklorist', James G. Delaney, *The Past*, No. 14, 1983, p. 55.

49   *Legends of Mount Leinster* - Preface by Kevin Whelan, Duffry Press, Enniscorthy, 1989.

50   Joseph Sheridan Le Fanu (1814–73), b. 45 Dominick St, Dublin, 24 August 1814. Ed. at TCD. Called to the Irish Bar 1839. Owner of three newspapers: *The Warder; The Evening Packet*; and *Dublin Evening Mail* amalgamating them as the *Evening Mail*. Editor and proprietor of the *Dublin University Magazine* from 1869–72. d. 7 February 1873 at his residence Merrion Square South, Dublin. *A Dictionary of Irish Biography*, Henry Boylan, Dublin 1978, pp.181–2.

51   *Wexford Independent*, 6 August 1851.

52   Jeremiah Curtin (1838–1906) b. Detroit, USA. Collector of Irish Folk Tales. Translator with US Government. d. Vermont USA. *A Dictionary of Irish Biography*, Henry Boylan, Dublin 1978, p. 77.

53   Douglas Hyde (1860–1949) translator, academic and President of Ireland. b. Castlerea, Co. Roscommon, Professor of Modern Irish at UCD. d. 12 July 1949, Dublin. *Modern Irish Lives* (ed. Louis McRedmond), Dublin 1996, pp. 141–2.

54   James Hamilton Delargy (1899-1980), b. Cushendall, Co. Antrim, M.A. in Celtic Studies, UCD. Assistant to Dr Douglas Hyde. He held the Chair of Folklore at UCD 1946–69. d. 1980. Article on Delargy by Michael McMahon, *The Other Clare*, Vol. 33, 2009, pp. 63–70.

55   *The Secular Priests of the Diocese of Ferns,* John V. Gahan, Editions du Signe, Strasbourg Cedex 2, France, 2000, p. 167.

56   The Roman Catholic Seminary was established in 1811 by Bishop Patrick Ryan (1768–1819) at Michael Street, Wexford. Dr Myles Murphy (1787–1856) prior to his elevation as Bishop of Ferns was appointed by Bishop Ryan as President of the Diocesan Seminary at Michael Street. *The Secular Priests of the Diocese of Ferns*, John V. Gahan, Editions du Signe, Strasbourg Cedex 2, France, 2000, pp. 402–3.

57   Bishop Patrick Ryan succeeded Dr James Caulfield (1732–1814) as Bishop of Ferns in 1814. In 1817 he purchased the house and land at Summerhill, Wexford and commenced work on what was to become St Peter's College and Seminary. St Peter's College opened in the autumn of 1819. *The Secular Priests of the Diocese of Ferns*, John V. Gahan, Editions du Signe, Strasbourg Cedex 2, France, 2000, p. 402.

58   Fr John V. Gahan gives a full account of this religious upheaval in his book which is worth recording in full and I quote verbatim: 'When he was appointed to the curacy of Enniscorthy, he found religious bigotry and intolerance rampant in the district. In 1826 the Orange Yeomanry had not been disbanded and the Orangemen paraded the town each succeeding year and subjected the Catholics to much insult. What was known as the "Liberty Tree" was erected in the Market Square, in the centre of a triumphal arch. The Yeomanry Corps subjected every Catholic that passed beneath it to maltreatment, if they did not bow to the "Liberty Tree". In 1839 the Yeomen used the butts of their carbines on Catholics who did not comply. Angered by this ill-treatment, the Catholics retired to the fair green to resolve a plan of action and were preparing to rush down on the Yeomanry Corps, regardless of all consequences when Fr Roche came upon the scene. He implored them to desist from the confrontation and succeeded in calming them. On his departure, however, some of the Orangemen insulted Fr Roche, and the people losing all restraint, rushed upon them with the cry "Down with Orangeism", "Away with the Liberty Tree", and a desperate conflict ensued. Fr Roche again exhorted the people to go to their homes, and after

repeated attempts he succeeded in restoring quiet. Such provocation was never repeated subsequently.' *The Secular Priests of the Diocese of Ferns*, John V. Gahan, Editions du Signe, Strasbourg Cedex 2, France, 2000, p. 366.

59   Rev. Dr John Sinnott P.P., born in Wexford town in 1790. Was appointed parish priest in the town and vicar general of the diocese on 13 March 1850, but never took office having been appointed as President of St Peter's College succeeding Dr Myles Murphy. Rev. Dr Sinnott died at the college 27 May 1850. *The Secular Priests of the Diocese of Ferns*, John V. Gahan, Editions du Signe, Strasbourg Cedex 2, France, 2000, pp. 364–5.

60   Richard Pierce, born c.1801 in Tenacre in the Parish of Kilmore, Co. Wexford. Married Ann Kelly of Wexford town and they had six children. Acted as Superintendent of Works for the Gothic form of architecture of Augustus Welby Northmore Pugin. In 1839, Pugin paid his first visit to Ireland for the laying of the foundation stone of St Peter's College chapel. Pugin came to rely on Richard Pierce's architectural talents to execute his church and building designs. By 1851, Pierce had his own architectural practice. By this time the foundation stones of the twin churches had been set and Pierce had been contracted to build the Church of the Assumption, Bride Street, Wexford. The contract price was £2,621 to be paid in instalments beginning at £283 8s when the foundations were at ground level. The second instalment of £309 7s 9d when the walls were at 7½ feet high with aisles and window sills in place. The third and fourth instalments of £494 1s 11d and £184 were paid when the sacristy and aisle walls were at full height. The final instalments were to be paid on completion of specified work as the building progressed. Augustus Welby Northmore Pugin died in 1852 aged 40 years, and Richard Pierce fell ill in 1854 and died in July of that year without seeing his churches completed. He was aged 53 years and is buried in Tomhaggard. The contractor for the Church of the Immaculate Conception, Rowe Street, Wexford was Thomas Willis. He had a similar agreement with Fr James Roche. In 1856, a former collaborator with Pugin, architect J.J. McCarthy, was commissioned to complete the outstanding work on both churches to Richard Pierce's specifications. 'Mr. Pierce of Tenacre', Celestine Rafferty, *The Twin Churches Book Wexford 1858–2008*, (ed. Eithne Scallan), Wexford 2008, pp. 1–4.

61   'Canon James Roche – Fundraiser Supreme and the Last Parish Priest of Wexford', Tom Williams, *The Twin Churches Book Wexford 1858–2008*, (ed. Eithne Scallan), Wexford 2008, pp. 5–9.

62   Architectural statistics of the twin churches: Each church is 166ft in length and 60ft in width. The towers are 16ft square with walls 5ft thick and 105ft in height. Octagonal tapering spires rise 222ft from the basement of the churches to the crosses on top. The distance between the two churches, main

door to main door is 560 yards. The wrought-iron church railings were made by Pierce's Foundry, Wexford.

The church bells: The bell in the Church of the Immaculate Conception is cast to sound the musical note of D and the bell in the Church of the Assumption is cast to sound the note of E. A peal of nine bells was erected in the tower of the Church of the Immaculate Conception in 1882 through the generosity of William Healy.

Rowe Street clock: The clock was installed in 1878 at a cost of £366.8.5 and was supplied by William Timpson, watchmaker and jeweller, 31 South Main Street, Wexford. *The Centenary Record of Wexford's Twin Churches 1858–1958* (ed. Matthew C. Bierney C.C.), Wexford, pp. 58; 100–101; 106.

Various other features: Outside the main entrance doors are unusual patterns in cobblestones often referred to as Wexford Mosaic. Furnishings are of handsome carved pews and nineteenth-century encaustic tiles on the floors. The stained-glass windows installed at the time of building would have been manufactured in England and Germany. A memorial window erected by the O'Keeffe family is a rare treasure and was designed by Ireland's foremost stained glass artist Harry Clarke (1889–1931). Both churches have magnificent three-manual Telford organs built in Dublin at the time the churches were built. The highly decorated organ pipes can be viewed from the body of the churches. The organs are still in use today and are a regular feature of church celebrations. Gleaned from informational leaflets available in several languages at the churches.

63   A native of Londonderry, Captain Robert McClure was born c.1775, 'an officer in the old 89th Foot and served abroad'. He saved the life of a fellow officer, General John Le Mesurier, a gentleman of considerable property and a native of Alderney, Channel Islands, who afterwards became guardian to his son. Capt. McClure, while stationed at Wexford with his regiment, married in 1807 Jane, daughter of Archdeacon Elgee. *The McClure family*, James Alexander McClure, published in Petersburg, Virginia, USA, 1914, p. 10.

64   One of the properties at No. 105 adjacent to a building which later became 'The New Hotel' on Foreshore Street (now Main Street) was occupied by Rev. Elgee and his wife. They had six children, one of whom was Charles. His daughter, Jane Francesca Elgee, known by her pen-name of 'Speranza', the poetess. Jane married Sir William Wilde and was mother of Oscar Wilde. *Unending Worship, A History of Saint Iberius Church, Wexford*, Norman Ruddock and Naomi Kloss, Impression Print, Wexford, 1997, pp. 14–5.

65   Charles Elgee was born in Durham in 1714 and was a bricklayer. He came to Ireland c.1730 with his brother, where there was a building boom. They settled in Dundalk, Co. Louth and quickly prospered. Charles' youngest son, John Elgee, was curate of St Iberius Church, Wexford from 1790 to 1794 and

rector from 1795 to 1823. Rev. John Elgee b. 1798 was appointed Archdeacon of Leighlin in 1804.

66 During my research, I failed to find a report on the actual location, date and cause of Captain McClure's death. He had served in Egypt with distinction at the Battle of Aboukir under General Ralph Abercromby, who fell mortally wounded, at the battle in 1801. Obviously, Captain McClure had returned to Ireland and was with his regiment at Wexford when he married Jane Elgee on 20 February 1806 at the Church of Castlebridge, as listed in the marriages section of the parish register.

67 *The Life of Vice-Admiral Sir Robert John Le Mesurier McClure C.B. Arctic Explorer and Discoverer of the North-West Passage (1807–1873)*, Andrew Dunlop, Rhodesia, 1975–76, p. 16.

68 *The Discovery of the North-West Passage by HMS 'Investigator' 1850, 1851, 1852, 1853, 1854*, Capt. R. McClure, Edited by Capt. Sherard Osborn, C.B. London, 1857. pp.18–20.

69 www.rmg.co.uk/discover/robert-mcclure-north-west-passage-expedition-1850.

70 The *Investigator* was a 'fast sailing' copper-bottomed A1 vessel doubled with wood all over, with bow and stern made to resemble the two ends of a caisson with wood and iron bolted over each other. In some places 29in thick of solid timber, coated in black paint with a white ribbon of paint and a small figurehead and described as ' not really a pretty vessel'.

71 *The Discovery of the North-West Passage by HMS 'Investigator'* … Capt. R. McClure, Edited by Capt. Sherard Osborn, CB, London 1857 pp. xxii–xxv.

72 Kabloonas (white men): the name by which the Esquinmaux called the visitors to their territory.

73 *The Life of Vice-Admiral Sir Robert John Le Mesurier McClure C.B. Arctic Explorer and Discoverer of the North-West Passage (1807–1873)*, Andrew Dunlop, Rhodesia, 1975–76, pp. 26–7.

74 https://www.rmg.co.uk/discover/explore/robert-mcclure-north-west-passage-expedition-1850

75 *The Wexford Independent*, 22 October 1853.

76 George LeHunte, Artramont, Castlebridge, Co. Wexford was one of 110 magistrates in the county. *Wexford County Guide and Directory*, George Henry Bassett, Dublin 1885, pp. 31–7.

77   *Wexford Independent*, 1855 – front page. Report edited by the author.

78   *The Life of Vice-Admiral Sir Robert John Le Mesurier McClure C.B. Arctic Explorer and Discoverer of the North-West Passage (1807–1873)*, Andrew Dunlop, Rhodesia, 1975–76, p. 41.

79   They had eleven children: Joanna, born 1844; Philip, 1846; Mary, 1884; Alice, 1852; Catherine, 1853; Anne, 1855; another Anne, 1856; Martin, 1858; James, 1859; another Alice, 1862; and John, 1864. 'Pierces of the Foundry', Hilary Murphy, *Kilmore Parish Journal* No. 18, 1989–90, pp. 3–5.

80   *ibid.*

81   *ibid.*

82   *A Century of Progress, 1839–1939*, Browne and Nolan, Dublin 1939, p. 24.

83   *River Slaney from Source to Sea*, John Duffy, published by John Duffy, Tullow, Co. Carlow 2006, p. 95.

84   *Wexford Independent*, 12 December 1868, which further commented on the death of James Pierce, 'we look on such a man as the lamented object of these passing remarks as an honour to the land of his birth, and an example to those blessed with the germ of intellectual power and steady perseverance must in the end conquer every difficulty.'

85   *Wexford – County Guide and Directory*, George Henry Bassett, Dublin 1885 (reprinted 1991, Dublin) pp. 115–8.

86   'Pierces of Wexford', Dr Austin M. O'Sullivan, *Wexford Historical Society Journal* No. 16 (1996–97), pp. 129–30.

87   'Pierces of the Foundry', Hilary Murphy, *Kilmore Parish Journal*, No. 18, 1989–90, pp. 3–5.

88   *ibid.*

89   'Pierces of Wexford', Dr Austin M. O'Sullivan, *Wexford Historical Society Journal*, No. 16 (1996–97), pp. 134/136/140.

90   *ibid.*

91   *Píob Mór*: mouth-blown war pipes not to be confused with the *uilleann* pipes. The Irish war pipes, by contrast, have been making a big noise across Europe for centuries. As long ago as 1581, Italian musicologist Vincenzo Gallilei – father of Galileo – wrote of the *piob mór*: 'The bagpipe is much used by the Irish. To its sound this unconquered, fierce, and warlike people

march their armies, and encourage each other to deeds of valour. With it also they accompany their dead to the grave, making such mournful sounds as to invite – nay, almost force – the bystanders to weep.' 'More Power to your Elbow, An Irishman's Diary', *Irish Times*, Friday, 12 January 2018.

92   *The Story of the Bagpipe*, W.H. Grattan Flood, London 1911, p. 114.

93   *Johnstown Castle – A History*, Liam Gaul, Dublin 2014, pp. 30–3.

94   Ballintore, Baile an Tóchair (townland of the causeway), Civil Parish: Kilbride; Barony: Scarawalsh; Union: Enniscorthy; DED: Ballymore; OS: 15, *Between Place and Parish* (compiled by Celestine Rafferty), Wexford County Council Public Library Service, 2004, p. 21.

95   John Cash, known as 'Cash the Piper', was born in Kilmore in March 1832. Cash served his time as a tinsmith, a trade which he combined with that of horse dealer. His enterprises made him a considerably wealthy man. John Cash grew up in an atmosphere of Irish music and learned to play the *uilleann* pipes from his uncle, James Hanrahan, a piper of repute. A frequent visitor to the home of Samuel Rowsome, of Ballintore, Ferns, himself an eminent piper, where many a long night's music was enjoyed. 'John and James Cash, pipers', Liam Gaul, *Kilmore Parish Journal*, No. 38, p. 91.

96   Frederick Jacob Blowitz was Music Master of Ferns Brass Band, County Wexford. Herr Blowitz lived in Ferns from 1878–85. *Wexford County Guide and Directory*, George Bassett, Dublin 1885, p. 336.

97   In piping, 'tipping' is a term used to describe a type of variation in which repeated staccato notes are used and 'tripling' is a form of ornamentation employed quite frequently with staccato fingering. Leo Rowsome stated, 'that the staccato notes must snap out like pistol shots'. *The Dance Music of Willie Clancy*, Pat Mitchell, The Mercier Press, Dublin and Cork 1976, p. 13.

98   Daniel O'Neill, familiarly known as Frank, was born 28 August, during the Great Famine at Tralibane, Co. Cork and was the youngest of seven children. he was taught to play the flute by a neighbouring gentleman farmer, Timothy Downing (c.1806–82). He settled in Edina, Knox County, Missouri where he qualified as a teacher in 1869. He married Anna Rogers at Bloomington, Illinois, a native of Feakle, Co. Clare. He joined the police force in July 1873 and began his music collecting activity in the city. He became General Supervisor on 30 April 1901. Chief O'Neill resigned in 1905 aged 57, having served thirty-two years' continuous police service. Captain O'Neill visited Ireland in 1906, his first journey home in forty years. He died of heart failure on 28 January 1936 and is buried in the family mausoleum in Mount Olivet Cemetery in Chicago. He published nine volumes of collected printed

musical notation and two textbooks. *A Harvest Saved, Francis O'Neill and Irish Music in Chicago*, Nicholas Carolan, Cork 1997, pp. 5–28; 62–5.

99   *Rí na bPíobairí* (King of the Pipers): the title of a vinyl LP record recorded by Leo Rowsome for Claddagh Records, the record label founded in 1959 by Guinness heir Garecht de Brún and Dr Ivor Browne to record and produce a record of their uilleann pipes teacher, Leo Rowsome, which was an appropriate title for such an eminent piper. *The Companion to Irish Traditional Music*, (ed.) Fintan Vallely, Cork University Press, Cork 1999, pp. 70; 323.

100   The Pipers' Club: The development of Irish music in Dublin can be traced mainly through the fortunes of the Dublin Pipers' Club from the period 1900 to the present day. From 1925 to 1936 the Pipers' Club in Dublin ceased to exist. The music continued to survive in the homes of the following musicians: William Rowsome and John Brogan (both pipe makers living in Harold's Cross), John Potts of The Coombe, and James Ennis of Finglas. In 1946 the Pipers' Club moved to Arus Ceannt, 14 Thomas Street. The identity of the Pipers' Club was eclipsed by the phenomenal growth of Comhaltas Ceoltóirí Éireann, founded in 1951 by members of the Pipers' Club at 14 Thomas Street. On October 14th, 1951, at Arus Ceannt, Thomas Street, Dublin, the first standing Committee of Cumann Ceoltóirí na hÉireann was elected. The premises at 14 Thomas Street were no longer adequate for the crowds attending each week. After much deliberation the Pipers' Club moved to a new premises located at Belgrave Square, Monkstown, in 1976 and is flourishing. https://comhaltas.ie/blog/post/history_of_the_pipers_club/

101   Fleadh Cheoil, a 'feast of music'. The first Fleadh Cheoil was held in Monaghan in 1952. Competitions are held in which people of all ages compete in many categories for instrumental music, song and dance. *The Companion to Irish Traditional Music* (ed.) Fintan Vallely, Cork University Press, Cork 1999, p. 134.

102   Walton's Musical Instrument Galleries, founded by Martin Walton c.1924. He started his business at the Dublin College of Music and opened his shop at North Frederick Street, Dublin. Martin Walton was a noted violinist and was a prize-winner at the Feis Ceoil. *The Companion to Irish Traditional Music* (ed.) Fintan Vallely, Cork University Press, Cork 1999, pp. 430–1.

103   The Fiddler of Dooney Competition originated in Sligo Town in the 1960s, and was organised by Paddy McGuire, Sean Forde, Paddy McSharry and others. The competition was held in Sligo Town until 1970, from 1970–72 it was held in Riverstown. It was in 1970 in Riverstown that the renowned piper, Leo Rowsome, died whilst adjudicating the competition. The current chapter in this competition's story is organised by the current Sligo Town branch of CCÉ. www.sligotowncce.com/fodwinners.html

104 The Potts Family: John Potts, an accomplished *uilleann* piper and native of Kiltra, County Wexford came to Dublin to seek employment, as did his brothers Tommy Potts, a fiddler, and Eddie Potts, a piper, fiddler and saxophonist. Their sister, Teresa, was an accordionist and pianist in the 1950s. https://en.wikipedia.org/wiki/Seán_Potts

105 *The Castles of County Wexford* (notes compiled from various sources), W. H. Jeffrey, private publication 1979.

106 *100 Wexford Country Houses, an illustrated history*, Dan Walsh, Enniscorthy 1996.

107 *Houses of Wexford*, Rowe, David; Scallan, Eithne (2nd edition), Clare 2016.

108 *Custos Rotulorum*: Keeper of the records. A principal justice of a county who keeps the Rolls or Records of the Sessions of the Justices' Court.

109 Charles Fitzgerald, 4th Duke of Leinster (1819–87) was an Irish peer and politician. He was born in Dublin and was son of Augustus Fitzgerald, 3rd Duke of Leinster and Lady Charlotte Augusta Stanhope. The duke was High Sheriff of Kildare for 1843 and Member of Parliament for Kildare from 1847 to 1852. He married Lady Caroline Sutherland-Leveson-Gower in 1847 at Trentham, Staffordshire. They had fifteen children including Gerald Fitzgerald, 5th Duke of Leinster (1851–93) and Lord Maurice Fitzgerald (Carton, 16 Dec. 1852 – Johnstown Castle, 24 April 1901).

110 George Arthur Hastings Forbes, K.P., 7th Earl, and a baronet. Born 5 August 1833 and succeeded his grandfather in 1837. He married Jane Colclough Grogan, youngest daughter of Hamilton Knox Grogan Morgan, Esq. of Johnstown Castle and had issue: Adelaide Jane Frances born 1860 and Sophia Maria Elizabeth born 1862. The family seat is Castle-Forbes, Longford. Their motto translates as: 'The incitement to glory is the firebrand of the mind'. *Debrett's Illustrated Peerage of the United Kingdom of Great Britain and Ireland 1865*, p. 169.

111 Col Harry Alcock, Wilton Castle, Enniscorthy and Charles M. Doyne, Wells, Gorey were both serving Deputy Lieutenants of County Wexford. *Bassett's Wexford County Guide and Directory*, George Henry Bassett, Dublin 1885, p. 31.

112 The County Wexford Society for Prevention of Cruelty to Animals had offices at 14 High Street, Wexford, Bassett, p. 41.

113 *ibid*. p. 41.

114 *ibid*. p. 41.

115 *ibid*. p. 45.

116 *Enniscorthy Guardian*, 20 April 1901, p. 5.

117 Horetown House is a Georgian square block country house standing three storeys above a basement situated 1.5 km approx. from the village of Foulksmills. It has 220 acres and the present appearance of the house is based on the plans of Wexford architect, Martin Day. Horetown was the family seat of the Goffs for many generations since 1693. The house was purchased by Major Lakin and proved to be the ideal area for hunting and other field events. *100 Wexford Country Houses*, Dan Walsh, pp. 57–8.

118 From the obituary of Lady Maurice Fitzgerald, *The People*, 21 November 1942.

119 *Wexford Connections: The Redmond Family and National Politics* (ed.) Celestine Murphy, Wexford Co. Council Public Library Service, 2018.

120 *The Wexford Gentry Vol. 1*, A. Kavanagh and R. Murphy, Bunclody, Co. Wexford 1994, pp.197–9.

121 *Walk Wexford Ways*, W. Roche; N. Rossiter; K. Hurley; T. Hayes, Wexford 1988, p. 29.

122 Notes circulated at a lecture – 'The legacy of John Edward Redmond' presented by Dr Martin O'Donoghue, NUIG at Redmond 100 Seminar, Wexford Library on Sunday, 15 April 2018.

123 Ballytrent House was purchased in 1799 by Walter Redmond, banker brother of John, founder of Redmond's Bank. This was the childhood home of John Edward Redmond and his brother Willie Redmond. *Wexford Connections: The Redmond Family and National Politics*, (ed.) Celestine Murphy, Wexford Co. Council Public Library Service, 2018.

124 'John Redmond – Parnellite and Nationalist', Dermot Meleady, *Journal of the Wexford Historical Society*, No. 21, 2006–07, p. 124.

125 *ibid.* p. 125.

126 *ibid.* p. 125.

127 *ibid.* pp. 126–8.

128 *John Redmond: The National Leader*, Dermot Meleady, Dublin 2014, p. 307.

129 *Wexford Connections: The Redmond Family and National Politics*, (ed.) Celestine Murphy, Wexford Co. Council Public Library Service, 2018.

130 *Our Town*, a series by Liam Gaul published by the County Wexford FREE Press, 2003.

131 Vignoles, O.J., 'Brief Sketch of the Career of Sir Robert P. Stewart', *Royal Musical Assoc. Proceedings of the Musical Association*, 24th Session (1897–98), pp. 318–9.

132 'Flood, Rev. William Grattan, Renowned Irish Musicologist', *The Capuchin Annual*, Dublin, 1974, p. 56.

133 Obituary: Wm H. G. Flood, *The Musical Times*, Vol. 69, No. 1027 (1 September 1928), London.

134 Grattan Flood, Wm H., *A History of Irish Music*, Browne and Nolan, Dublin, 1905, p. iv.

135 Grattan Flood, Wm H., *The Story of the Harp*, The Walter Scott Publishing Co., Ltd London, 1905.

136 Grattan Flood, Wm H., *The Story of the Bagpipe*, The Walter Scott Publ. Co., Ltd, London, 1911, pp. 1–2.

137 O'Byrne, Rev. S. (ed.), *The College Hymnal*, John English & Co. Ltd; Wexford, Hymn No. 35, 1964, p. 56.

138 Ferns Diocesan History and Archives Group, *Churches of the Diocese of Ferns*, Booklink, Dublin 2004, p. 25.

139 Gahan, Rev. John V., *The Secular Priests of the Diocese of Ferns*, Editions du Signe, France, 2000, p. 162.

140 Dearmer, P., Williams, R.V., Shaw, M. (eds.), *The Oxford Book of Carols*, OUP, London, 1928, pp. 30–1.

141 Ó Tuama, Seán Óg, An Chóisir Cheoil, Uim. 1, Comhlucht Oideachais na hÉireann, Áth Cliath, 1964, p 3.

142 *102 Years of Wexford I.C.A.*, Enniscorthy, County Wexford 2012, pp. 8–9.

143 *ibid*. pp. 8–9.

144 Bree An Bhrí (the hill), Civil Parish of Clonmore in the Barony of Bantry and the Enniscorthy Union. DED: Bree; OS: 25. Bree is located in the centre of County Wexford – 52° 26' 06' N   6° 36' 18' W. Porta tomb (Dolmen Intrepid United Irishwomen) is nearby at Ballybrittas on Bree Hill.

145 *Those Intrepid United Irishwomen*, Sarah McNamara, Limerick, 1995, pp. 40–1.

146 *ibid*. pp. 40–1.

147   *Women of Wexford 1798–1998*, Anna Kinsella, Dublin 1998, p. 81.

148   The Queen Victoria Jubilee Institute for Nurses was set up by private subscription. The Jubilee Nurses travelled around bringing nursing care to the sick and infirm in their homes. Their usual outer dress was a long grey or black overcoat and they travelled the country lanes by bicycle or pony and trap. See *Jubilee Nurse*, Elizabeth Prendergast and Helen Sheridan, Wolfhound Press, Dublin 2012.

149   *Women of Wexford 1798–1998*, Anna Kinsella, Dublin 1998, p. 82.

150   *102 Years of Wexford I.C.A.*, Enniscorthy, County Wexford 2012, pp. 8–9.

151   *Women of Wexford 1798–1998*, Anna Kinsella, Dublin 1998, p. 83.

152   *Those Intrepid United Irishwomen*, Sarah McNamara, Limerick 1995, pp. 60–3.

153   *Women of Wexford 1798–1998*, Anna Kinsella, Dublin 1998, p. 97.

154   *ibid*. p.79.

155   *Those Intrepid United Irishwomen*, Sarah McNamara, Limerick 1995, pp. 60–3.

156   The first Holy Confraternity Brass and Reed Band existed from 1895 to 1910 and the second band was formed in 1926. *The Twin Churches Book Wexford 1858–2008*, Eithne Scallan, Wexford 2008, p. 81.

157   Three Bullet Gate is situated on the south-eastern corner of the town of New Ross directly in front of Talbot Hall. During the Insurrection of 1798 the Bantrymen were chosen to carry out the assault on Three Bullet Gate. The force was to be lead by John Kelly of Killann. His instructions were to take the gate itself and hold it until other battalions joined them. Following this attack the entire combined forces were to push forward into the heart of New Ross. *The People's Rising, Wexford 1798*, Daniel Gahan, Dublin 1995, p. 122.

158   *Tales of the Anvil – The Forges and Blacksmiths of Wexford*, Eamon Doyle, Nonsuch, Dublin 2008, p. 53.

159   Jem Clarke made his debut as a lightweight boxer on 13 September 1898 and won his fight in five rounds by a knockout. Clarke was a Dubliner.

160   Jem Roche fought Jack Fitzpatrick on 25 August 1900 at the Ancient Concert Rooms in Dublin. Roche won in the fourth round by a KO to attain the Heavyweight Championship of Ireland. Report by Tracy Callis, historian, International Boxing Research. www. cyberboxingzone.com/ boxing/roche-jem.htm

161 Nicholas J. Tennant was proprietor of a pawnbroking shop in Wexford town and served as manager to Jem Roche. Tennant's had several pawn shops in the town including a premises at George Street, which was eventually incorporated into the business of Herbert Coffey.

162 Report by Tracy Callis, historian, International Boxing Research. www. cyberboxingzone.com/boxing/roche-jem.htm

163 *Tales of the Anvil*, Eamon Doyle, pp. 23–8.

164 Tommy Burns: the professional name of Noah Brusso (born 17 June 1881, Hanover, Ontario, Canada – died 10 May 1955, Vancouver, British Columbia), Canadian World Heavyweight Boxing Champion from 23 February 1906, when he won a twenty-round decision over Marvin Hart in Los Angeles, until 26 December 1908, when he lost to Jack Johnson in fourteen rounds in Sydney, Australia. This victory made Johnson the first black fighter to hold the heavyweight championship, a development that outraged some fans and even led to rioting in the United States. Burns had successfully defended his title eleven times before the fight with Johnson. From 1900 to 1920 Burns had sixty bouts, winning forty-six, thirty-six by knockout. Near the end of his boxing career, Burns joined the Canadian army and taught boxing to military recruits. He was also involved in various business ventures, including a clothing store and a speakeasy. Late in his life Burns underwent a religious conversion, and in 1948 he became an ordained minister. Despite the large sums he had made during his career, Burns died impoverished. He was inducted into *Ring* magazine's Boxing Hall of Fame in 1960. Tom Humphries in the *Irish Times*, Saturday, 21 June 2008 – www.irishtimes.com/ wexford-footballers-have-had-a-few-jems-down-the-years

165 Richard Croker (1843–1922) was born in the village of Blackrock, Cork in County Cork, on 24 November 1843. He was taken to the United States by his parents when 2 years old. Richard was educated in the public schools of New York City, where he eventually became a member of Tammany Hall and active in its politics. As head of Tammany, Croker received bribe money from the owners of brothels, saloons and illegal gambling dens. He survived Charles Henry Parkhurst's attacks on Tammany Hall corruption and became a wealthy man. www.rte.ie/..../ radio-documentary-richard-croker-ireland-tammany-hall-new-york.htm

166 This report was written by William Redmond for *The People* newspaper following the St Patrick's Day 1908 contest between Jem Roche and Tommy Burns, and was reprinted in the same newspaper as part of an obituary for Jem Roche, 8 December 1934.

167 *Tales of the Anvil*, Eamon Doyle, pp. 23–8.

168 William Redmond's report in *The People* newspaper as part of Jem Roche's obituary, 8 December 1934.

169 *Main Street – Heart of Wexford*, Nicky Rossiter, The History Press, U.K. 2018, p. 39.

170 *Enniscorthy Echo*, 1 December 1934.

171 *Tales of the Anvil*, Eamon Doyle, pp. 23–8.

172 From correspondence with James Gaul, a Wexfordman domiciled in Cobh, Co. Cork, and I quote: 'James Gaul's Grandfather was Richard Roche, Clifford Street, Wexford, Garage proprietor, and brother-in-law of Jem Roche, the boxer. Richard stated that Jem Roche was the strongest man he knew, yet he died at 57 years of age of Gangrene as a result of a neglected in-growing toe nail and not, as reported, from an accident. Richard Roche used to promote bouts in the Theatre Royal between boxers from Belfast and local Wexford boxers.'

173 *Eileen Gray – her work and her world*, Jennifer Goff, Sallins, Co. Kildare 2015, p. 15.

174 https://www.independent.ie/lifestyle/visionary-gray-shines-strong-29135137.html

175 *Eileen Gray – her work and her world*, Jennifer Goff, Sallins, Co. Kildare 2015.

176 www.independent.ie/life/home-garden/interiors/98-facts-about-eileen-gray

177 *Eileen Gray – her work and her world*, Jennifer Goff, Sallins, Co. Kildare 2015, p. 15.

178 Jean Badovici (1893–1956), his real name was Badoviso, was born in Bucharest on 6 January 1893 and he became a naturalised French citizen in the 1930s. He died in Monaco on 17 August 1956. He began his academic studies at the School of Fine Art supervised by Julien Guadet and Jean-Baptiste Paulin and graduated at the Ecole Spéciale d'Architecture. In 1924, Badovici contributed to *Wendingen* where he devoted an entire issue to Eileen Gray. It was Badovici who first mentioned Eileen Gray to Le Corbusier. On his death the UAM paid tribute to him at the Museum of Decorative Arts.

179 *De Stijl*, the design magazine that Theo van Doesburg founded in November 1917, became the term for Dutch modernism. *Wendingen*, its chief competition, was not so lucky. Founded three months later by the architect and graphic designer H. Th. Wijdeveld as the mouthpiece for the Amsterdam School of architects and designers, it is largely forgotten, despite its important influence on modern typography. www.nytimes.com/2001/07/20/arts/art-in-review-wendingen-dutch-design

180   The Bibendum chair was a take on the Michelin Man which had tyre-like shapes sitting on a chromed steel frame.

181   www.independent.ie/life/home-garden/interiors/98-facts-about-eileen-gray

182   www.independent.ie/life/home-garden/interiors/98-facts-about-eileen-gray

183   *The Daily Telegraph*, 25 February 2009.

184   *Eileen Gray – her work and her world*, Jennifer Goff, Sallins, Co. Kildare 2015, pp. 21–5.

185   *More Irish Families*, Edward MacLysaght, Dublin 1982, p. 33.

186   *Families of County Wexford*, Hilary Murphy, Wexford 1983, pp. 50–2.

187   Oral interview with Helen Corish-Wylde.

188   *ibid.*

189   In the engineering works or iron foundries the various departments or sections were referred to as shops, i.e. the Machine Shop, the Wood Shop, the Pattern Makers Shop, etc.

190   See Davitt; Connelly; Larkin and Collins – *100 Irish Lives* by Martin Wallace, David & Charles, London 1983.

191   *Richard Corish, A Biography*, Kieran S. Roche, Original Writing, Dublin 2012, p. 11.

192   Oral interview with Helen Corish-Wylde.

193   *Men of Iron, Wexford Foundry Disputes 1890 and 1911*, Michael Enright, Wexford Council of Trade Unions, 1987, pp. 22–4.

194   *Richard Corish, A Biography*, Kieran S. Roche, Original Writing, Dublin 2012, pp. 19–51.

195   Oral interview with Helen Corish-Wylde.

196   In the author's interview with Helen Corish-Wylde she recounted how her father's (Des Corish) brother, Brendan, was convinced that their father was not allowed back to work in any of Wexford's foundries as he was perceived as a troublemaker by the employers and that this was a condition of the final settlement to end the lockout. Some men emigrated because of the lockout.

197   In a letter written by Richard Corish to Jim Larkin, Liberty Hall, Dublin on 8 July 1912 on the headed paper for the Irish Foundry Workers' Union,

he concludes his letter with a P.S.: 'I shall send you the insurance forms by Thursday.' Letter in the personal collection of Helen Corish-Wylde.

198 The 'Ancient Order of Foresters' was founded in 1834 as a British benevolent society giving benefits, such as health insurance, with membership by subscription. In 1877, however, the breakaway Irish National Foresters was founded by members who were expelled by the British leadership for having become involved in the amnesty campaign. It expanded rapidly to have a total of 1,000 branches and 250,000 members worldwide by the 1910s, wherever Irish emigrants gathered in numbers. The Foresters in their ceremonial garb were a familiar sight to Irish people of the day at 'national' events such as Bodenstown, Ivy Day (for Parnell's memory) or the funeral of O'Donovan Rossa. An abbreviation of a letter to the *Irish Times*, Monday 17 July 2017, from David Flood, Drumcondra, Dublin 9.

199 The title of Honorary Freeman of Wexford is granted under the Municipal Privilege Act of 1876 and can only be given by a majority vote of those who attend a statutory meeting for the purpose of discussing the merits of a nominee. The meeting must have a total agreement on the choice of candidate as one dissenter will prevent acceptance of the person to be honoured. All recipients must come to Wexford for the ceremony, a rule which has been adhered to since 1881. Two members of the Corish family were added to this illustrious list of Honorary Freeman of Wexford, Alderman Richard Corish, TD in 1945 and his son, Brendan Corish, TD in 1984.

200 Oral interview with Helen Corish-Wylde.

201 *Richard Corish, A Biography*, Kieran S. Roche, Original Writing, Dublin 2012, pp. 100–1.

202 https://stairnaheireann.net/2013/11/19-1918-labour-party-leader-brendan-corish/

203 *Wexford – A Municipal History*, Padge Reck, Wexford 1987, p. 115.

204 Oral interview with Helen Corish-Wylde.

205 *ibid*.

206 *Wexford – A Municipal History*, Padge Reck, Mulgannon Publication, Wexford 1987, p. 48.

207 *The Chronicles of the County Wexford to the year 1877*, George Griffiths, Enniscorthy 1890, pp. 289–478.

208 Morriscastle (Caisleán Mhurcha - Murcha's Castle), Parish of Kilmuckridge, barony of Ballaghkeen N, Gorey, Co. Wexford.

209   *Songs of the Wexford Coast*, Fr Joseph Ranson, Enniscorthy 1948, pp.102–3.

210   The Faythe is an area in Wexford town renowned for its many navigators and sailors who left from the quayside under canvas heading for such ports as Odessa on the north-western shore of the Black Sea and Galatz, an inland port c.120 miles north-east of Bucharest in sea voyages that could last for several months. As 'going to sea' was one of the few employments available to young men, the Christian Brothers School taught navigational skills to those students who proposed taking to the world's oceans, giving them the opportunity for advancement.

211   *Songs of the Wexford Coast*, Fr Joseph Ranson, Enniscorthy 1948, pp. 13–4.

212   Castletown, (Baile an Chaisleáin) in the Parish of Kilgorman in the Barony of Gorey, Co. Wexford.

213   Donoghmore (An Domhnach Mór), in the Barony of Ballaghkeen N, Gorey, Co. Wexford.

214   The *Alfred D. Snow* bound from San Francisco with a cargo of grain for Liverpool was wrecked on 4 January 1888. There were only seven bodies found from a crew of twenty-nine. The eleven-verse song was composed by famous ballad-maker Michael O'Brien and is sung to a variant of 'The Felons of Our Land'.

215   'Bannow's Lonely Shore' is a descriptive song of yearning by an emigrant for his own native place. It was composed by John Kane, a native of Grange, Bannow, while in exile in America. The air is a variant of 'Gleann Beag Lách an Cheoil' known in Wexford town as 'Carrig River'.

216   'The Fethard Lifeboat Crew' is a song of the tragic loss of nine crew of fourteen that manned *The Helen Blake* lifeboat in their attempt to rescue the captain and crew members of a stricken vessel wrecked on the Keeragh Rocks. Fr Ranson collected four versions of this ballad in his book. See *The Awful Tragedy of the Helen Blake Lifeboat, Fethard. Co. Wexford 1914* by Liam Ryan, New Ross, Co. Wexford 2010.

217   The *Hantoon*, a barque owned by Richard Devereux, Wexford, was lost on the homeward voyage from Galatz, 27 December 1881. The vessel was 'run down' by a British ship off the coast of Portugal. This song was recorded from Margaret Mitten in 1937. The ballad was composed by William Martin, Slippery Green, Wexford. The air to this ballad was transcribed from the singing of James Mahony, Bride St, Wexford by Miss Kathleen Grattan Flood in 1947.

218   'The Mexico' tells the tale across its twelve verses of the wreck of this Norwegian schooner on 20 February, 1914. She was sailing from Lithuania to Liverpool with timber for the docks. The captain was a Norwegian and not a Mexican as stated in verse two, and was Captain O.E. Ericksen.

219   The *Pomona* set sail from Liverpool on 27 April 1859 'bound for the land of plenty' (America) with a crew of thirty-five and 400 passengers. The ship wrecked on Blackwater's Banks following a raging storm. All hands and passengers were lost including Irish artist, Sir John Lavery's father. It is possible that the *Pomona* was named after the Roman goddess of fruit or a city in south-west California or the Latin name for fruit (*pomum*). Fr Ranson published two versions of this ballad, the second of which he believes not to be pertaining to the *Pomona* but to a ship called the *Georgiana* and factually incorrect. See p. 109 of *Songs of the Wexford Coast*.

220   *The Secular Priests of the Diocese of Ferns*, John V. Gahan, Strasbourg Cedex 2, France, 2000, pp. 163–4.

221   The Theatre Royal, known as the venerable 'old lady' of High Street, operated as a playhouse from 1832 to 2006, a total of 174 years, when its doors closed for the last time and the building was completely demolished. A totally new state-of-the-art theatre, now the National Opera House, replaced the Theatre Royal built by William Taylor, whose family owned and published the *Wexford Herald* at their offices on Main Street. The Theatre Royal opened its doors to the public on 4 January 1832. *A Window on the Past*, Liam Gaul, p. 29.

222   Signor Adelio Viani, musician and singing teacher at the Royal Irish Academy of Music, Dublin was born c.1890 in Milan, Italy. He held the Diploma of Composition from the Royal Conservatorio of Milan and was Professor of Singing at the Conservatorio and Professor of Piano in the Calchi-Taeggi. In 1932 Maestro Viani was honoured by the King of Italy with the title of Cavalier of the Crown of Italy. In 1917 Adelio Viani was appointed Professor of Singing at the Royal Irish Academy of Music, a position he held for almost fifty years. He encouraged an operatic tradition in Dublin and in 1928 founded the Dublin Operatic Society where he was Musical Director. In 1945 he published a series of musical essays in his book, *Towards Music*. Maestro Cavalier Adelio Viani, his wife, Florence and daughter, Countess Maria Viani Nolan are buried in the family plot in St Brigid's Cemetery, Dean's Grange, County Dublin. See *Music in Ireland*, (ed.) Aloys Fleischmann, Cork University Press, 1952, pp. 244–5 and *Dungarvan Leader and Southern Democrat*, Saturday, 15 December 1945, front page.

223   Dublin-born Michael William Balfe (1808–70), Irish composer and singer was the son of a dancing master. A talented youth, he was playing the violin, aged 7, at his father's classes. The Balfe family lived in Wexford for a short time

in 1810 where his father gave dancing classes at the Assembly Rooms above the Market House in Cornmarket, a building which now serves as Wexford Arts Centre. It was with Balfe's opera, *The Rose of Castile*, that Dr Tom Walsh chose to launch the Wexford Festival, thanks mainly to the composer's links with the town. *What the Doctor Ordered*, Kevin Lewis, p. 30.

224 Dr T.J. Walsh published the following books relating to opera covering eighteenth-century Dublin, opera in Monte Carlo and the Second Empire in Paris as follows: *Opera in Old Dublin 1819–1838*, Free Press, Wexford 1952; *Opera in Dublin 1705–1797,* Allen Figgis, 1973; *Monte Carlo Opera, 1879–1909*, Gill and Macmillan, Dublin 1975; and *Second Empire Opera: The Théâtre Lyrique Paris 1851–1870* (History of Opera series), Calder Pubs Ltd, 1981.

225 Michael O'Hehir: A broadcaster and sports commentator, best known for covering Gaelic games and horse racing. Michael O'Hehir gave his first commentary on 14 August 1938, when Galway defeated Monaghan in the All-Ireland football semi-final. His voice was to become synonymous with radio coverage of hurling and football, and his broadcasts were important to the thousands of people who gathered around radio sets in the 1940s and 1950s in Ireland and abroad. He covered major GAA matches from 1938 until 1985, when illness prevented him from covering his 100th All-Ireland final. O'Hehir began commentating on horse racing in 1947, and went on to work for the BBC and ABC in America. O'Hehir's skills as a commentator took him in a different direction in November 1963. A trip to New York with his wife coincided with the assassination of US President John F. Kennedy. The responsibility to comment on the funeral on behalf of Telefís Éireann fell to O'Hehir and his coverage won him praise in both Ireland and the US. Michael O'Hehir died in Dublin in November 1996. rte.ie/ archives/exhibitions/1411-radio-sports.../1452-michael-ohehir/

226 *Cúchulainn's Son, the Story of Nickey Rackard,* Tom Williams, Dublin 2006, p. 2.

227 *ibid.* pp. 6–7.

228 Christy Ring was born on 30 October at Kilboy, Cloyne in 1920. As a youngster he showed great hurling promise and at 14 he won his first medal with Cloyne. He later won a county minor medal with St Enda's (1938) and a county junior medal with Cloyne (1939). He starred with the Cork minors in their All-Ireland win of 1938 and, while still a teenager, he played with the Cork juniors and seniors in 1939. He captured his first league medal with Cork in 1940 and he was chosen for Munster a year later. He established many championship records, including career appearances (65), scoring tally (33-208) and the number of All-Ireland medals won (8). Ring is widely regarded as one of the greatest hurlers in the history of the game, with many former players, commentators and fans rating him as the number one player

of all time. In 1956 he was deprived of the ninth All-Ireland medal by Art Foley's famous save for Wexford. He played his last game for Cork in June 1963. Ring was most famous for his scoring prowess, physical strength and career longevity. He remains the only player to have competed at inter-county level in four different decades. Christy Ring died suddenly on 2 March 1979 and the scenes which followed at his funeral were unprecedented in Cork since the death of the martyred Lord Mayor Tomás Mac Curtain in 1920.

229 Slaneysiders: a collective name applied to all Wexfordians and comes from the name of the River Slaney which flows down thorough the county.

230 County Wexford's first All-Ireland hurling victory came in 1910, their only one in that code until seventy-one years later following the establishment of the Gaelic Athletic Association. In this match Wexford failed to score a point, which never happened before or since with any other championship team. The players that represented County Wexford were mainly from Castlebridge with only three members of other clubs. Wexford achieved victory over Castleconnell, Limerick at Jones' Road, Dublin on 20 November. Seating was provided at the venue for the first time with chairs being provided on the sideline. The final score was 7 goals to 6 goals and 2 points. *With the Gaels of Wexford*, published by Sean O'Faolain, Enniscorthy, December 1955, p. 27.

231 Leesiders: a collective name applied to all Corkonians and comes from the name of the River Lee which flows down thorough the county.

232 *Cúchulaínn's Son, the Story of Nickey Rackard*, Tom Williams, Dublin 2006, p. 118.

233 Alcoholics Anonymous.

234 The late Tom Williams, a native of Taghmon, County Wexford, was a historian, author and songsmith. He contributed articles to many historical journals and newspapers. He researched and wrote seven genealogical books on Wexford families and was author of *With Heart and Hand, the Inside Story of Wexford's Hurling Resurgence* and *Fairways of the Sea – 100 Years of Golf at Rosslare*. Tom was a founding member and served as President of Taghmon Historical Society and also was Chairman of Innovation Wexford. A collection of his poems and songs, *A Voice from Out the Crowd*, was published posthumously by the Williams family. Permission to quote some lyrics from Tom's song was granted by David Williams, his son.